B
FREUD   Muckenhoupt,
              Margaret.

          Sigmund Freud.

                              11BT02771
$11.95

DATE			

BAKER & TAYLOR

Owen Gingerich
General Editor

Sigmund Freud

Explorer of the Unconscious

Margaret Muckenhoupt

Oxford University Press
New York • Oxford

To my grandmothers, Sarah Muckenhoupt and Kathryn Heath, my husband Scott, and Hajime, my one-time muse.

Oxford University Press

Oxford   New York
Athens Auckland Bangkok Bogotá Buenos Aires
Calcutta Cape Town Chennai Dar es Salaam Delhi
Florence Hong Kong Istanbul Karachi
Kuala Lumpur Madrid Melbourne Mexico City
Mumbai Nairobi Paris São Paulo Singapore
Taipei Tokyo Toronto Warsaw
and associated companies in
Berlin Ibadan

Copyright © 1997 by Margaret Muckenhoupt
Published by Oxford University Press, Inc.,
198 Madison Avenue, New York, New York 10016

Oxford is a registered trademark of Oxford University Press

Design: Design Oasis
Layout: Leonard Levitsky
Picture research: Laura Kreiss

Library of Congress Cataloging-in-Publication Data
Sigmund Freud / by Margaret Muckenhoupt.
p. cm. — (Oxford portraits in science)
Includes bibliographical references and index.
ISBN 0-19-509933-8 (cloth); ISBN 0-19-513212-2 (paper)
1. Freud, Sigmund, 1856–1939—Juvenile literature.
2. Psychoanalysis—Austria—Biography—Juvenile literature.
[1. Freud, Sigmund, 1856–1939. 2. Psychoanalysis.]
I. Title. II. Series
BF109.F74M83 1996
150.19'52'092—dc20   95-42340
                              CIP

9 8 7 6 5 4

Printed in the United States of America
on acid-free paper

Frontispiece: *Freud, holding his customary cigar, in a 1929 portrait*

Contents

Chapter 1. Origins 9

Chapter 2. Experiments 26

              Sidebar: The Rise and Fall of Hypnosis 40

Chapter 3. Conversations 43

              Sidebar: Strong Medicine 47

Chapter 4. Explanations 54

              Sidebar: Katharina's Cure 63

Chapter 5. Departures 67

Chapter 6. Solutions 81

Chapter 7. Interactions 90

Chapter 8. Reality 105

Chapter 9. Struggles 121

Chapter 10. Exhaustion 134

Epilogue 147

Chronology 150

Further Reading 152

Index 155

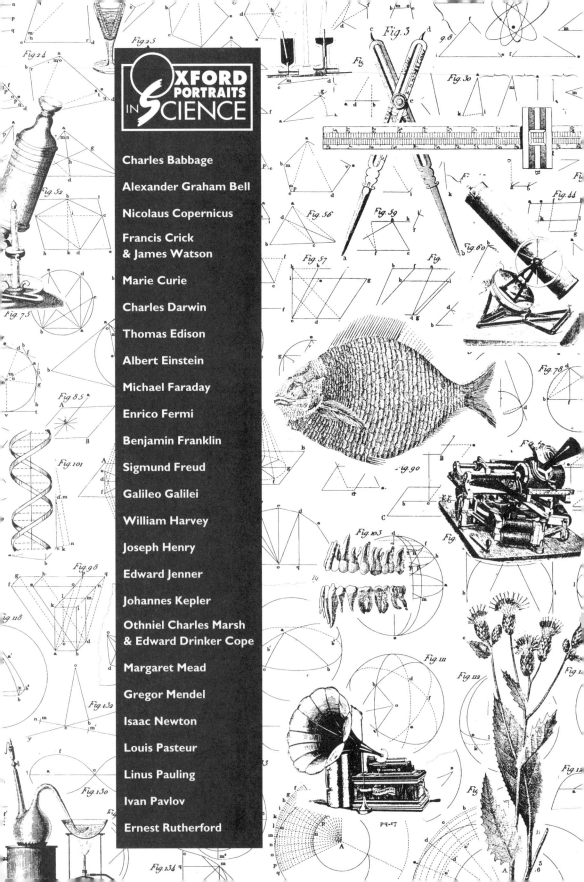

OXFORD PORTRAITS IN SCIENCE

Charles Babbage

Alexander Graham Bell

Nicolaus Copernicus

Francis Crick
& James Watson

Marie Curie

Charles Darwin

Thomas Edison

Albert Einstein

Michael Faraday

Enrico Fermi

Benjamin Franklin

Sigmund Freud

Galileo Galilei

William Harvey

Joseph Henry

Edward Jenner

Johannes Kepler

Othniel Charles Marsh
& Edward Drinker Cope

Margaret Mead

Gregor Mendel

Isaac Newton

Louis Pasteur

Linus Pauling

Ivan Pavlov

Ernest Rutherford

In the course of the centuries the naive self-love of men has had to submit to two major blows at the hands of science. The first was when they learned that our earth was not the center of the universe but only a tiny fragment of a cosmic system of scarcely imaginable vastness. . . . The second blow fell when biological research destroyed man's supposedly privileged place in creation and proved his descent from the animal kingdom and his ineradicable animal nature. . . . But human megalomania will have suffered its third and most wounding blow from the psychological research of the present time which seeks to prove to the ego that it is not even master of its own house, but must content itself with scanty information of what is going on unconsciously in its mind. . . . Hence arises the general revolt against our science, the disregards of all considerations of academic civility and the releasing of the opposition from every restraint of impartial logic.

—Sigmund Freud, on opposition to psychoanalysis,
Introductory Lectures on Psycho-Analysis (1933)

After Freud fled Vienna for the safety of London in 1938, he managed to create an exact replica of the office he had had in his home in Vienna, which was filled with ancient artifacts.

Origins

The entrance to the doctor's office is quite ordinary. He lives and works in a middle-class neighborhood in Vienna, in an apartment house on a quiet city street. You climb the stairs to the residence bearing the name "Prof. Dr. Freud," open the door, and walk into a waiting room. Promptly, the doctor appears for your appointment. He is of medium height, about five feet seven, a bit stooped over, and dressed like a very neat and proper university professor. Yet his dark brown eyes are shining and bright; they seem to pierce you. With an air of authority, he instructs you to enter his chambers.

When you walk into the consulting room, you gasp; in this small, dark room, the doctor has created a miniature museum. You stride across a darkly patterned oriental rug and gaze at the treasures that surround you. To your left, you see shelves and shelves of figurines: Egyptian gods molded in pale, dry clay, a camel with two humps, Greek heads with unseeing eyes and curling hair, calm cross-legged Buddhas, coiled snakes, and chalices. You are tempted to pick one up, but somehow you sense that every object is in its exact place, and that the professor would notice if anything were moved. Everywhere you look, the walls are crowded with fragments of ancient paintings, mosaics, and stones. In front of you is a couch, with one end raised so that patients may recline comfortably. The couch is covered with yet another exotic rug and several pillows. The doctor sits down on a chair behind the head of the couch and motions for you to lie down. You cannot see the doctor from the couch; you can only admire his antiques. As you lie back on the pillows, you are faintly aware of the aroma of cigars and of coal smoke from the stove. You had imagined that this consulting room would be plain and functional like other doctors' offices—a place covered in white sheets and smelling of disinfectant and strong soap. What sort of doctor treats you in a gallery of relics?

When most people think of psychotherapists, the image that comes to mind is that of Freud, silently sitting, observing, and smoking a cigar while a patient lies on a couch and talks about his mother. Very few scientists have been as widely influential, or as commonly condemned, as Freud. Freud's theories of love, language, power, human development, and death are studied throughout the world and applied to disciplines ranging from psychology to anthropology to literary theory. Still, whenever Freud's work is studied, fierce debates begin.

Psychoanalysis, the therapy Freud developed for treating mental illness, has been criticized as being both too dangerous and completely ineffective. His writings on children's sexuality and the "death instinct" have horrified many critics. Freud has been faulted for making vague claims that could not be scientifically proved, for emphasizing the sex drive above all other human motivations, and for using his own experience as the model for human psychological development.

Some of these charges are valid. Others represent a misunderstanding of both the theory and the man. Freud did not simply dream up psychoanalysis after reading too many paperback potboilers. Sigmund Freud was a professionally trained scientist whose study of mental illness was based on widely accepted 19th-century doctrines of biology. Most important, there is no fixed Freudian creed. Freud's ideas evolved over his lifetime, and he continued to revise his theories until his death. His followers have reviewed and expanded his work and are still doing so today.

Freud did not intend his methods to be transparent to the world. Though he frequently used examples from his own life in his work, Freud was an intensely private man. He burned his old notebooks, diaries, and manuscripts in 1885 and again in 1907. During the first round of destruction he wrote to his fiancée: "As for the biographers, let them worry, we have no desire to make it too easy for them. Each one of them will be right in his opinion of 'The Development of the Hero.'" Despite his efforts, enough of Freud's letters and manuscripts have survived to show that while he may not have been a hero, he was a brilliant researcher and a scientific revolutionary. Freud was not a beast, and not a god, but a brave and fascinating man.

Sigismund Schlomo Freud was born to Amalia and Jacob Freud on May 6, 1856. The Freuds lived in the town of Freiberg in Moravia, a part of the Austro-Hungarian Empire that today lies within the Czech Republic. Freiberg (now known as Príbor) was a small town of 5,000 people. When Sigismund was born, his family lived in a single rented room on the second floor of an unassuming house, over a blacksmith's shop. At the time, most Jews in Moravia were poor and lived in cramped quarters. Jacob Freud grew up in Galicia, a province of the Austro-Hungarian Empire that is now divided between Poland and the Czech Republic. He left home when he was 29 and traveled to Freiberg, where he joined his grandfather as a cloth merchant. In 1859, when Sigismund was three, the family moved to Leipzig, Germany, for a year, and then on to Vienna, the capital of the Austro-Hungarian Empire. By then, the Freuds had a second child, Sigismund's sister Anna. In the next six years, the Freud family swelled with the arrival of four more daughters, Adolfine, Marie, Pauline, and Rosa, and a second son, Alexander.

Sigismund spent his first three years surrounded by golden meadows and green woods, with the Carpathian Mountains looming in the distance. He never forgot his beloved Freiberg, and when he was 75 he wrote, "Deep within me, covered over, there still lives the happy child from Freiberg, the first-born son of a youthful mother, who had received the first indelible impressions from this air, from this soil."

Vienna, by contrast, made a dreadful impression on him. Writing to his friend Wilhelm Fliess in 1900, Freud proclaimed, "I am as hungry as a young man for the spring, and sun, and flowers and a stretch of blue water. I hate Vienna with a positively personal hatred and, just the contrary of the giant Antaeus, I draw fresh strength whenever I remove my feet from the soil of this city which is my home." In Vienna, Freud encountered anti-Semitism, severe antagonism toward Jews, and suffered repeated professional failures and rebukes. Yet he lived there from the age of 5 until he was 82. Vienna was Freud's home. He was dislodged only by the Nazi invasion of Austria in 1938.

When Sigismund was born, Jacob was 40 years old and Amalia was 21. Amalia was a very beautiful woman, and she was proud of her looks. At the age of 90, she refused to buy a hat that a daughter offered her, shouting, "I won't take this one; it makes me look old!" Her grandchildren variously described her as a "tyrant" or a "tornado," a passionate woman who did not restrain her fury. In a letter to his fiancée, Sigismund claimed that his mother gave him his "sentimentality"—his passionate temperament and fierce emotions.

Jacob, by contrast, was even-tempered but ineffectual. He was a tall, broad-shouldered man and read the Bible at home. Sigismund later thought that he was physically and mentally his father's duplicate. Jacob Freud was always optimistic, but he was never very successful in business, and in later years he became incapable of supporting his family. When Sigismund was 28, he wrote an appeal to Jacob's sons from an earlier marriage, Philipp and Emanuel, asking them to bail their father out of his financial predicament.

Jacob had been raised as an Orthodox Jew and read and spoke Hebrew fluently. However, he ignored most religious observances and treated holidays such as Purim and Passover as family celebrations instead of religious holidays. He even hired a non-Jewish nursemaid for his firstborn son. Sigismund later claimed that his father "allowed me to grow up in complete ignorance of everything that concerned Judaism." This statement is not strictly true: According to his autobiography, Sigismund began to read the Old Testament when he had "barely acquired the art of reading," but he never learned to read Hebrew.

Freud's mother, Amalia, remained a strong influence on Freud until her death at the age of 95.

Sigismund was disappointed in his father, whom he perceived as weak. One of his most vivid childhood memories was his father's story of an incident that had occurred when he was a young man. While Jacob was taking a walk, a Christian had knocked a brand-new cap off his head and shouted, "Jew, off the sidewalk!" When Sigismund asked his father what he had done, Jacob replied, "I stepped into the road and picked up my cap."

Sigismund was not happy with his father's response. In school, he studied the deeds of heroes. He was eternally fascinated with Moses, the Jewish prophet who led his people out of slavery in Egypt and delivered the Ten Commandments to them at Mount Sinai. Sigismund named his toy soldiers after Napoleon's generals. He also idolized Hannibal, the North African general who brought his army across the Alps to the gates of Rome. For Sigismund, Hannibal symbolized the outsider challenging the established power of Rome (as the Jews had to challenge Roman Catholics, who made up the majority of Vienna's population). In later life, Freud physically confronted anti-Semites, yelling angrily and charging with his walking stick at those who shouted and taunted him.

It is not clear how Jacob Freud made his money once he got to Vienna; his name does not appear in trade directories or in lists of businessmen paying taxes at the time. Jacob may have borrowed money from his wife's relatives and from Philipp and Emanuel, his grown sons from his first marriage, in order to survive. He was able to support Amalia and his seven children comfortably, though, giving them books and tickets to the theater, having his children's portraits painted, and paying Sigismund's full tuition at school. Amalia suffered from tuberculosis and made regular summer excursions to resorts in the Carpathian Mountains to restore her health. In 1865, Jacob's brother, Josef, was convicted of trading in counterfeit money. It is possible that Jacob, Philipp, and Emanuel were involved in Josef's schemes, which certainly would have helped buoy the Freuds' finances.

Sigismund was indulged. His mother called him "my golden Sigi" until she died at 95. Older relatives often told him that when he was born, an old peasant woman told Amalia that she had just "given the world a great man." On another occasion, the 12-year-old Sigismund was told by a strolling poet that he would become a cabinet minister. When Sigismund began attending university in 1875, he was given his own room at home, while the other eight members of the family squeezed into the remaining three bedrooms. Freud's family was willing to make sacrifices for the bright firstborn son.

Freud's Jewish background had profound implications for both his intellectual development and his life in society. When Austria annexed Galicia in 1772, the number of Jews in Austria increased from 70,000 to almost 300,000. Austrian leaders responded to this situation by passing laws that would reduce the Jewish population. Jews had to pay a high poll tax, or risk being expelled from their hometowns. A high marriage tax prevented many Jews from marrying, except in secret, and Jewish children were required to go to German schools. Until 1848, Austria maintained strict laws concerning where Jews could live. In Moravia, Jews could only live in 52 designated Jewish communities and were only permitted to stay in the big towns and cities if they were declared "tolerated Jews" by the local authorities, who imposed a "toleration" tax upon them.

In 1848, Europe was racked by revolution. In France, Germany, Croatia, Hungary, Austria, and parts of Italy, citizens demanded that their autocratic governments become modern republics, with a free press and democratic elections. Most of these popular movements were crushed by the ruling monarchs and emperors.

In Austria, though, the liberals were given limited power under a centralized government ruled by Emperor Franz Josef. A parliament called the Reichsrat was established in Vienna. The imperial cabinet (a group of advisors to Emperor Franz Joseph) was filled with ordinary middle-class politicians instead of landed aristocrats, and committees quickly composed, revised, and jettisoned 8 different constitutions in 20 years. The Austrians were trying to create a new nation that relied on laws, democratic elections, and secular, or nonreligious, authority to replace the old state ruled by the monarchy and the Catholic church. They had mixed success.

The Austrian liberals never had much support beyond the middle-class Christians and Jews in the large cities, and they stayed in power by limiting the right to vote to men who had money and were likely to support them. In 1873, only 6 percent of Austrian adult males could vote. However, the liberals' legal reforms were very important to Freud and his family. By 1867, when Sigismund was 11 years old, not only had Austrian liberals eliminated the anti-Jewish laws; several Jews had even joined the government. As Sigismund later recalled, it was a time when "Every diligent Jewish boy carried a minister's portfolio in his satchel." He was well aware that his good fortune was due to the liberals' reforms, and he loyally supported them.

As Jews' fortunes rose, so did the Jewish population in Vienna. Families flocked to the capital city. In 1857, there were 6,000 Jews in Vienna; by 1867, there were 40,000, amounting to 6 percent of the population. Some Jews were descended from "tolerated" Viennese families, spoke German, and fit well into Viennese culture; others, like the Freuds, came from small towns in the hinterlands.

Unlike many of the poorer Jews, though, the Freuds spoke standard German at home, not Yiddish, a German dialect spoken by most eastern European Jews. The Freuds, like many other Jewish families, tried to assimilate into the Christian middle class. In the wake of Austria's liberal reforms, Jewish students entered the professions as quickly as possible. By the 1880s, Vienna's Jewish population rose to 72,000, 10 percent of the total, and more than half the city's lawyers, doctors, and journalists were Jewish. Viennese Jews were also active in the arts, banking, and education.

This is not to say that anti-Semitism had disappeared from Vienna. Sigismund had to put up with anti-Jewish taunts from his classmates at the gymnasium, his secondary school, and his later career was also hampered by discrimination. Still, during his youth and early adulthood, Viennese Jews were hopeful, and Sigismund was able to work without much fear of discrimination.

Sigismund grew up immersed in biblical history. In later life, he filled his writing with Old Testament references and often wrote on the Bible's psychological implications. However, he became a staunch atheist (a person who does not believe in any god) early on, and remained one throughout his life. His feelings on the issue were so strong that as an adult he banned all Jewish observances from his home, much to his wife's dismay. (Yet Freud wrote in his autobiography, "My parents were Jews, and I have remained a Jew myself.") He worried, as psychoanalysis became more popular, that it would be viewed as a discipline that interested only Jews, and he worked strenuously to encourage non-Jews to spread psychoanalysis throughout society. These efforts did not impress the Nazis when Adolf Hitler's army invaded Austria in 1938. All Jews, religious or not, were in danger of being sent to concentration camps and killed, and Freud was forced to leave Vienna.

As the child of a third marriage, the young Freud misunderstood his family's structure. Jacob Freud had married Amalia Nathansohn in 1855, when he was 40 and she was 20. Jacob's sons from his first marriage, Emanuel and Philipp, were far closer in age to Amalia than Jacob was. Emanuel was older than Amalia, whereas Philipp was only a year younger. One of Sigismund's first playmates was Emanuel's son John; Sigismund was actually John's uncle, but he was a year younger than his nephew. Naturally, Sigismund believed that his half brother Philipp, a bachelor, was much better suited to marry Amalia than his father, Jacob. But Jacob was Amalia's husband. When

A Freud family portrait in 1876. Sigmund (back row, third from left) stands next to his half brother Emanuel, one of his father's sons from his previous marriage.

Freud's younger sister Anna was born, Sigismund worried that Philipp had taken his father's place and given his mother a child.

At the same time Sigismund was experiencing confusion about his young, beautiful mother, he was also being cared for by an old Czech nursemaid. This nurse seemed like a much more natural match for Jacob than Amalia. An enthusiastic Catholic, the nursemaid would sneak Sigismund off to church. Amalia later told her son, "When you got home, you would preach and tell us what God Almighty does." Many researchers believe that this nanny was the source of Freud's fascination with Rome, the residence of the Catholic pope. As a nursemaid, she was also responsible for Sigismund's bathing and toilet training. He enjoyed his nanny's attentions and recalled her vividly when he began to dredge up forgotten childhood memories in the 1890s.

Like all children, Sigismund had mixed feelings about his siblings. When his brother Julius was born, Freud was 17 months old and intensely jealous. Julius died seven months later. Sigismund's first sister, Anna, arrived several months afterwards, again usurping his position as the only child; he never liked Anna very much in later life. When Sigismund was two and a half, his half brother Philipp accused Freud's nursemaid of theft, and she was arrested, convicted, and sent to prison. Sigismund was quite upset, as any small child would be. When Freud later theorized about family relations, he remembered these rivalries very clearly.

The Vienna of Freud's childhood was a vibrant, booming metropolis. The number of businesses and the population in Vienna had doubled between 1840 and 1870. In 1857, Emperor Franz Josef declared that the huge circle of open land that surrounded the city, formerly the site of gigantic fortifications, should be developed for civilian use. This tract became Vienna's grand boulevard, the Ringstrasse (literally, "Ring Street"). When the Ringstrasse was dedicated in 1865, it was immediately filled with vast apartment houses and public buildings. In the next two decades, Vienna rapidly constructed an opera house, museums, a parliament building, and a town hall, as well as a dizzying variety of cafés.

Vienna in the late 19th century was prosperous, and the city became a cultural center for art, music, literature, and, importantly for Freud, medicine. By the end of the century, luminaries like the artist Gustav Klimt, composers Gustav Mahler and Arnold Schoenberg, writers Arthur Schnitzler and Hugo von Hofmannsthal, and dozens of other intellectuals were enriching Viennese culture. Freud did not take much advantage of these urbane delights; he did not care for the avant-garde writers, artists, and composers of the day, and he never enjoyed lolling about in coffeehouses. Aside from his daily walk, Freud's principal joy in Vienna was its museum.

Freud began his education in Vienna. At first, his father taught him at home. Freud then attended a private primary school, and entered the gymnasium, a combined middle/high school, at the age of nine. He was at the head of his class for six out of his eight years at the gymnasium. As he grew up, Freud devoured reams of classical literature from ancient Greece and Rome, learning Latin and Greek as well as French and English (he taught himself Spanish and Italian on the side). Freud also read Shakespeare's plays in English. An avid reader even in his youth, he took it upon himself to censor his sister's books. He told Anna, then 15, that she could not read the works of the French writer Honoré de Balzac, author of a series of novels titled *The Human Comedy,* because they were too racy. It was natural that by the end of his teenage years, he would go on to study at the University of Vienna.

At first, Freud planned to become a lawyer. In his autobiography, he states, "Under the powerful influence of a friendship with a somewhat older Gymnasium colleague who later became well-known as a politician, I too wanted to study law and become socially active." He changed his mind by the time he began his college studies, though. Freud later claimed that he decided to become a scientist when he heard a popular lecturer and zoologist named Carl Brühl read a passionate poem about Nature, the Embracing Mother. Freud wanted to study nature. One way to do that was to study biology.

In the autumn of 1873, Freud enrolled as an under-graduate medical student at the University of Vienna. Here he changed his name from Sigismund to Sigmund. He committed himself to at least 10 semesters (5 years) of medical studies. He later wrote that he "felt no particular partiality for the position and activity of a physician in those early years, nor, by the way, later. Rather, I was moved by a sort of greed for knowledge." Young and ambitious, Freud also had a greed for fame. He would stroll around the campus, looking at the statues of great professors, foreseeing that one day he, too, would stare out over the students, contemplating eternity. He imagined his own bust would feature a quotation about Oedipus, the mythical Greek who won a kingdom by answering the riddle of the Sphinx: "He divined the famous riddle and was a most mighty man" (from the ancient Greek dramatist Sophocles' play *Oedipus Rex*). Freud simply had not yet settled on which riddle to solve.

Freud was fascinated by the biologist Charles Darwin's controversial theory of natural selection, which Darwin had introduced to the world in 1859. In *The Descent of Man,* published in 1871, Darwin stated that humans, like other organisms, were subject to evolution, and had descended from "a hairy, tailed quadruped"—an animal. Many people believed (and many still believe) that this idea was an insult to both humans and God. However, Freud and his fellow scientists saw Darwin's theories differently.

While Freud was a medical student at the University of Vienna, he became fascinated with the controversial theory of natural selection put forth by English biologist Charles Darwin (above).

A theory that says "God created this fish" cannot be tested. But if a theory states, "This fish was selected because it survives better than its ancestors," then scientists have many puzzles to solve. What other fish is this fish related to? How is it different? What organs are the same? When did the change happen? Did other types of animals, like frogs, or dolphins, undergo the same changes? Why was this change useful? Was there some difference in the environment that could have caused this change?

In short, Darwin's theories made modern biology possible. It is hard to describe the enormous effect Darwin had on biological research. When Freud attended the University of Vienna, biologists were searching for evidence of evolution everywhere. As Freud later wrote, "The doctrines of Darwin, then topical, powerfully attracted me because they promised an extraordinary advancement in our understanding of the world." And Freud, the secular atheist, who detested irrational thought, was probably pleased that Darwin's theory of the origin of species disposed of God.

Freud also delved into the work of the philosophers Ludwig Feuerbach and Franz Brentano. Feuerbach wholeheartedly opposed most philosophy and theology (the study of religious doctrine), claiming that theology should be replaced by anthropology, the study of human evolution and development. Theology is merely a reflection of human experience, Feuerbach wrote—an argument Freud made over and over again decades later in his books *The Future of an Illusion* and *Totem and Taboo*. While devouring Feuerbach's books, Freud attended five courses of lectures and seminars taught by Brentano, who termed himself an "empirical psychologist," that is, a psychologist who studies the mind through observation and experiment. A former priest, Brentano was concerned with how the mind worked, not what information it acquired. He was also a scientist who retained his faith in God, a position that Freud found intriguing. In addition, Brentano was an expert on the ancient Greek philosopher Aristotle and his impact on the science of psychology.

In his third year, Freud settled into a laboratory devoted to physiology, the study of the functioning of living organisms and their components, such as tissues, organs, and cells. The laboratory was run by Ernst Brücke, an eminent Viennese scientist. Freud worked there for the next five years. Over the course of his life, Freud adopted many different men as father figures, wise guides to whom he owed the utmost loyalty. Brücke was one of the first. He was 40 years older than Freud, about the same age as Jacob Freud.

But in contrast to the cheerful, passive, good-humored Jacob, Brücke was a reserved, demanding taskmaster. When Brücke was present at students' oral exams, he would ask only one question. If the student did not know the answer, Brücke would ask no more questions and would sit silently until the full 15-minute exam was over. When the rigid and authoritarian Brücke discovered that Freud was arriving late to the laboratory, he stood outside the door at opening time and waited. Freud never forgot "the terrible blue eyes with which he looked at me and before which I melted away," an image he recalled in his book *The Interpretation of Dreams*. Yet Freud adored Brücke, who gave him a sense of professional self-discipline. Like so many other professors of the time, Brücke had strong cultural interests as well. He was a gifted painter and invented a universal phonetic

Freud spent five years working in the laboratory of Ernst Brücke, studying physiology. Freud considered Brücke his chief mentor and left his laboratory only when he was forced to find a more lucrative position.

writing system that he claimed could be used for transcribing all languages.

Professionally, Brücke was part of a group of scientists who had dedicated themselves in the early 1840s to combating vitalism, a school of biology that explained the life activity of organisms through a mysterious vital force. This vital force was supposed to be immaterial, like a sort of soul. Brücke and his colleagues firmly believed that only physical and chemical forces affected organisms. Any action of a living being or its organs could be reduced to chemical or physical laws. The anti-vitalists, through careful experimentation, made great progress in physiology and the study of how human perception changes due to variations in physical stimuli, like the brightness of light. When he left Brücke's laboratory, the idea that any biological phenomenon could be reduced to physical laws was firmly fixed in Freud's mind. Much later in his career, when Freud explored the causes of human behavior, he sought explanations based on observations of physical processes to account for the channeling of mental energy.

Working with Brücke, Freud published papers on the structure of the nervous systems of fish and crayfish, as well as the structure of eels' sex organs and a novel method of separating them from other tissues.

Freud spent eight years taking his degree, three years longer than the average for medical students. In 1879, his studies had been interrupted when he was drafted, and he spent a year in peacetime military service, tending to sick soldiers. Yet Freud showed that he was capable of working rapidly while in the army. During that year, he translated four essays by the philosopher John Stuart Mill from English into German, a commission he received through a recommendation from his old teacher Franz Brentano.

After he passed the qualifying examinations for his medical degree, Freud took a poorly paid post as a teaching assistant at Brücke's Physiological Institute. He left the institute only when he had no other choice. Freud was not slow or unintelligent, but he had no good motive for leaving a laboratory where he enjoyed the research and could work productively. However, Brücke could not support an eternal student. Freud may have been patiently waiting to be awarded an assistantship in Brücke's lab. Unfortunately, both of Brücke's assistants were young and unlikely to leave their posts. Also, money was becoming increasingly important to Freud. He had met a young woman named Martha Bernays in April 1882 while she was visiting one of his sisters. Two months later, Freud and Bernays were engaged. They lacked the money to set up a household, however, and Brücke took the opportunity to tell Freud that he could never expect to support a wife through research. Within six weeks of his engagement, Freud began work as an entry-level intern at the General Hospital in Vienna.

Experiments

Martha Bernays was just the woman to make Sigmund Freud's head spin. Intelligent and attractive, she was 21 years old when the couple met in April 1882; Freud was 26. Bernays's family was overwhelmingly intellectual. Her grandfather, Isaac Bernays, had been the chief rabbi of Hamburg, and two of her uncles taught at German universities. Her father, Berman, was a merchant and also worked as secretary to a famous Viennese economist, Lorenz von Stein. The Bernays family had come to Vienna from Hamburg, Germany, in 1869, when Martha was eight, and the Freud and Bernays families had become friendly. Martha often visited the Freud sisters, and Martha's brother Eli married Sigmund's sister Anna in 1883.

Martha herself was by all accounts not an intellectual, though she was properly educated for her time. She was familiar with German literature and was an avid reader—but only in the evenings. She never allowed herself such a frivolous pastime during the day, when there was work to be done. There is little record of her thoughts about her engagement to Freud; her letters to him will not be released to the public until the year 2000. In later years, though, she showed her talent for calm, efficient, and fiercely proper household management. She tolerated and resisted Freud's jealousies during their engagement (as his letters to her indicate), and she later managed the Freud household, which included six children and a number of servants, with patience and care.

Martha was secure and not easily ruffled. She could control her emotions to the point of seeming cold. Her son Martin later recalled an instance when he fell against a piece of furniture and cut his head, producing cascades of blood. Martha did not cry out or even put down her sewing. Instead, she simply asked the governess to call the doctor, who lived on the same street, and kept sewing.

Martha Bernays in 1884, two years before her marriage to Freud.

During her marriage, Martha was a quiet and efficient administrator. As she once said, "I shun any kind of publicity. I believe in the proverb that the best wife is the one about whom the least is said." In essence, she lived independently from her husband; he gave her the household allowance, and she ensured that dinner appeared promptly at 1 P.M. Martha never bothered to learn very much about Freud's work and generally did not travel with him on vacations that did not include the children. She also conducted her social life separately, diplomatically smoothing over relations with friends and relatives whom Freud had insulted. She also ignored Freud's demands that she drop certain individuals, such as her friend Elise, who, as Martha delicately phrased it, had "married before her wedding."

When Freud met Martha Bernays, though, all he saw was a slender, pale, lovely young woman. Martha had almost married an older businessman, but her brother Eli talked her out of it, arguing that she should marry only if she were in love. On the fateful night in April 1882, Martha was visiting the Freuds when Sigmund came home from work at the university. Usually, Sigmund marched straight to his room to study. That evening, though, he saw Martha talking and laughing with his sisters. The young man was entranced. He wrote in a letter to Martha years later that he was becoming superstitious "since I learned that the first sight of a little girl sitting at a well-known long table talking so cleverly while peeling an apple with her delicate fingers could disconcert me so lastingly." The family was stunned when Sigmund sat down at the table and joined the conversation. He did so every time Martha appeared. Within a few weeks, Sigmund was sending Martha a rose every day. The stern censor, devoted student, and rational scientist was calling Martha Bernays "the fairy princess from whose lips fell roses and pearls." Sigmund loved her desperately from the moment they met.

Unfortunately, neither Freud nor Bernays had enough money to get married. For a variety of reasons, they delayed informing their families of their engagement for six months. During that time Martha's mother decided to move back to Hamburg, even though Martha's sister Minna was also engaged to a Viennese man. Bernays and Freud were forced to live in different cities for three of the four and a half years of their engagement. This was not entirely unusual at the time; Martha's own mother had been engaged for nine years. Still, for Freud it was a time of exquisite torture.

To stay in touch, Freud and Bernays exchanged letters every other day. Freud's letters display his devotion and his demands. He insisted that his fiancée be cool to her admirers and ordered her to call a cousin by his last name instead of his first name. He even demanded that she give up ice skating; otherwise, she might lose her balance and lean on another man's arm. He expressed his belief that giving the vote to women was absurd, considering their responsibilities in the home. He required Martha to give up her religion, Orthodox Judaism, upon marriage. Martha did stop practicing Judaism, though she was profoundly disturbed by Sigmund's demand. After he died, she lit the traditional candles marking the Jewish Sabbath every Friday night.

Occasionally, Freud also described their future home, a perfect place of middle-class comfort:

> All we need is two or three little rooms where we can live and eat and receive a guest and a hearth where the fire for cooking does not go out. And what things there will have to be: tables and chairs, beds, a mirror, a clock to remind the happy ones of the passage of time, an armchair for an hour of agreeable day-dreaming, carpets so that the Hausfrau [housewife] can easily keep the floor clean, linen tied up in fancy ribbons and stored on their shelves, clothes of the newest cut and hats with artificial flowers, pictures on the wall, glasses for the daily water and for wine on festive occasions, plates and dishes, a larder when we are suddenly overcome with hunger or a guest arrives unexpectedly, a large bunch of keys which must rattle noisily, and the friendly lamp. And everything must be kept in good order, else the Hausfrau, who has divided up her heart into little bits, one for each piece of furniture, will object.

In another letter, Freud commented, "I have the impression that the dearest woman in the world is mortal on that point and regards a husband as a supplement—a necessary one, it is true—to a beautiful home."

Supporting a wife and home takes money. Six months before their marriage, as they tried to scrape together the money to furnish their home, Freud wrote to Bernays, "Oh, my little darling, you have but one minor fault; you never win the lottery." When he left Brücke's laboratory, Freud simply did not have any cash. He was also three years behind his contemporaries, who started practicing medicine immediately after earning their degrees. From 1882 to 1885, Freud worked hard to gain the experience he needed to practice clinical medicine. He rotated through most of the medical departments, including surgery, dermatology, and ophthalmology, as well as psychiatry and nervous diseases. Yet Freud also wanted to make a great scientific discovery. If he found some exciting new result, he would become famous; if he were famous, he would have a large private practice; and if he had a large private practice, he would have enough money to wed Martha Bernays without delay.

Because of his eagerness to marry, Freud's beloved Martha indirectly caused one of his greatest scientific defeats. In his quest for fame he tried a new method of staining tissue—the process of dying cells so that they would be easier to see under a microscope—using gold chloride, but his technique did not produce consistent results. He also published a paper on a patient who had a cerebral hemorrhage (bleeding in the brain), but even this failed to bring him recognition. He needed a better idea. To be able to marry his "tender, sweet girl"—as he had addressed her in his letter proposing engagement—Freud began to investigate cocaine.

In the early 1880s, cocaine use was not as widespread or notorious as it is today. Scientists had not researched the drug's properties. Freud became interested in cocaine after reading a German army doctor's report that the drug increased soldiers' endurance. Like many other researchers of the day, Freud decided to test this new drug on himself. He had his reasons. For many years, Freud had suffered from bouts of depression. He would become tired, irritable, and unable to work. When he sampled small doses of cocaine, he found that it helped him work with new energy. Freud was delighted. As he wrote to Martha, "And if you are disobedient you shall see who is stronger, a gentle little girl who doesn't eat enough or a big wild man *who has cocaine in his body.* In my last severe depression I took coca again and a small dose lifted me to the heights in a wonderful fashion. I am just now busy collecting the literature for a song of praise to this magical substance."

Freud himself did not suffer any side effects from the drug, and he proceeded to publish a paper titled "On Coca" (the plant from which cocaine is derived) in July 1884. Freud recommended cocaine as a local anesthetic and as a cure for exhaustion, stomach ailments, and morphine addiction. He even mailed samples of the drug to Bernays, recommending that she dose herself when she seemed out of sorts.

Freud's enthusiasm was his downfall. In the summer of 1884, he mentioned cocaine's numbing properties to two ophthalmologist friends, Leopold

Sigmund Freud in 1885, shortly before he traveled to Paris to study with French doctor Jean-Martin Charcot.

Königstein and Carl Koller. Freud even gave a dose of cocaine to a fellow medical intern, who reported that the drug made his lips and tongue numb. Freud and Königstein started experimenting with the effects of cocaine on a dog's eye. However, the research was interrupted by Freud's summer vacation in July.

Freud immediately rushed to see Bernays, whom he had not visited for a year. When he returned in September, he found that Koller, not Königstein, had performed and reported experiments on using cocaine as a local anesthetic on the eye. To be fair, Koller had been trying to find a local anesthetic for use in eye surgery for some time before Freud gave him the inspirational dose. Koller's discovery transformed eye surgery and brought him instant fame. Freud remained a poor, young, unknown—and unmarried—doctor.

Cocaine's influence on Freud's life did not end with this academic disaster, though. He had prescribed cocaine to a friend, Ernst von Fleischl-Markow, as a cure for morphine addiction. With the help of Freud's drug, Fleischl-Markow did manage to stop taking morphine. However, he soon became addicted to cocaine and continued to abuse the drug until his death in 1891. While Fleischl-Markow was dissolving his body and mind with daily injections, medical reports of cocaine addiction began to arrive from all over the world. Freud came under attack for his cocaine enthusiasm, and he finally abandoned the topic altogether. However, he continued to take the drug himself occasionally for several years, to help him tolerate parties during his time in Paris, to combat migraine headaches and stomach pains, and to ease nasal swelling. Unfortunately, cocaine may have made Freud's migraines and nasal troubles much worse.

Fortunately, Freud had kept himself busy while experimenting with cocaine. His work as a hospital doctor, and the energetic support of his old adviser Brücke, earned Freud a travel scholarship. In the fall of 1885, he left Vienna to visit his beloved Martha. From there, he journeyed to Paris to study with the French medical celebrity Jean-Martin Charcot for five months at the Salpêtrière Hospital.

Charcot had charmed the French nation through the use of hypnotism. In the 1870s, he headed a large hospital ward of patients who suffered from what was then called grand mal epilepsy, a disease of the nervous system marked by seizures. During these seizures, the patients would lose consciousness, turn very pale, foam at the mouth, and have convulsions. The ward was also occupied by patients who did not suffer from epilepsy but had learned to imitate the seizures. This second set of patients were said to suffer from hysteria.

Hysteria has had many definitions over the centuries. The term itself has roots in the Greek word for womb (also the source for the word *uterus*) and was thought to be a disease of women's reproductive organs from the time of ancient Egypt through the 19th century. The ancient Greeks had a detailed theory of hysteria. They believed that a woman who had no sexual relations, generally a widow or spinster, would experience changes in her womb. The womb, or uterus, would dry up, become lighter, and float upward in the body. If the womb happened to settle in the throat, the woman would feel a lump in her throat, and might have problems breathing. The Greek physician Hippocrates wrote, "When a woman suffers from hysteria or difficult labor an attack of sneezing is beneficial," perhaps to push the uterus back to its original location.

In the 16th century, various anatomists demonstrated that the womb was very firmly attached to the body and was unlikely to travel. An English physician named Thomas Sydenham stated that "antecedent sorrows," or psychological traumas, were the cause of hysterics' suffering. However, hysteria was still seen as a woman's disease. By 1813, the Frenchman Philippe Pinel, a physician famous for freeing institutionalized mental patients from their chains during the French Revolution, charged that hysteria was the result of sexual deprivation in women. When the deprived woman was emotionally unstable and had indulged herself sexually in other ways (by reading pornography, for example), she would develop hysteria. To cure the disease, he recommended that victims suffering irregular menses have regular menstruation be restored through a variety of treatments, and that women have sexual intercourse with their husbands before winter.

By the time Freud entered medical school, not much had changed. Hysteria was no longer strictly a women's disease—there were many reports of male victims—but it was

During the latter part of the 19th century, many scientists, including Freud, tested cocaine on themselves. However, researchers quickly became aware of the dangers posed by use of the powerful drug. This poster for a French play dramatizes some of the risks associated with the drug.

still commonly viewed as a result of frustrated sexual desires. Many doctors saw it as an expression of women's inherent flaws. After all, weren't women dominated by their passions and inherently unstable? Others observed that hysteria was a very successful way to rebel against the imposed responsibilities of womanhood. A woman who was unhappy at being treated purely like a mother and housekeeper, toiling at maintaining the home and constantly attending the needs of her husband and children, could not leave her position very easily. Instead, she could get sick. Free from housework, with the children whisked away and a worried husband ordering doctors and drugs, the hysterical woman could control her household yet be free of her hated duties. Of course, the victim never intended to be sick, or tried to produce symptoms. She was "speaking through the body," saying with her illness what she could not express directly.

Some doctors suggested horrifying surgical treatments or "rest cures" during which the patient was separated from her family, put to bed in a dark room, and not allowed to leave her bed for a month. Whatever its causes, hysteria does seem to have been mostly a women's disease in the 19th century, with very few male victims. After World War I, the ailment virtually disappeared. Researchers still debate why this happened. Some point out that social conditions changed. Others claim that 20th-century doctors have simply stopped diagnosing hysteria as an illness, though many patients continue to show "hysterical symptoms."

Freud's experience with hysteria was defined by two French physicians, Charcot and Paul Briquet. In 1859, Briquet took a bold step and actually surveyed the symptoms of 430 hysterical patients housed at the Hôpital de la Charité in Paris. He found two facts that

In the fall of 1885, Freud traveled to Paris to study with Jean-Martin Charcot, a French doctor who had amazed the people of France with his use of hypnotism. Freud was fascinated by Charcot's techniques and later used hypnosis when treating his own patients.

contradicted the sexual hypothesis: first, that 1 man suffered from hysteria for every 20 female patients; and second, that while nuns rarely suffered from hysteria, many prostitutes did. Clearly, sexual deprivation was not the cause. Briquet stated that hysteria was a disease of the nervous system, defining it as "a neurosis [nervous disease] of the brain, the manifestations of it consisting chiefly in a perturbation of those vital acts which are concerned with the expression of emotions and passions." According to Briquet, hysteria emerged when sensitive people were overwhelmed by violent emotions.

Charcot and Briquet believed that hysterics would exhibit seizures when they felt strong emotion or when they were under stress. However, these seizures were distinct from epileptic seizures. Charcot and an assistant outlined four stages of a hysterical attack and used these criteria to distinguish between true epileptics and hysterical patients. The four stages were the "aura," or premonition of the attack; the attack itself, when the patient screamed, lost consciousness, and suffered convulsions; a "clownish" phase, when the patient would make expansive gestures that looked like theatrical expressions of grand emotions; and resolution, when the patient would cry or laugh. Charcot was fascinated by the apparent purpose behind these attacks; the patients looked like they were trying to communicate something. He was also intrigued by the way the attacks resembled reports of demonic possession, of spirits trying to enter the body. Charcot, like Freud, was eager to demonstrate that all manner of demons, spirits, and witches could be explained away by science.

Apparently, the hysterical patients did not realize that they were not physically ill, that they did not suffer from epilepsy. In much the same way, hypnotized patients could not remember the instructions given by a hypnotist after they came out of trances. Charcot consequently became interested in the ways that ideas that are not accessible to normal consciousness can affect the mind. In the 1880s, he was principally concerned with hysterical paralysis. This form of paralysis did not produce the same symptoms as physical paralyses. For example, Freud himself observed that while physical paralyses were generally more severe in parts of the body farthest from the trunk—the feet and hands—in hysterical paralysis the shoulders might be more severely affected. Freud later wrote that hysteria "behaves as though anatomy did not exist or as though it had no knowledge of it." In other words, hysterical paralysis manifests itself the way people *believe* a paralysis is supposed to act, not the way it actually does.

It was a short leap for Charcot to go from investigating hysteria, where a patient does not know that he or she is ill, to studying hypnotism, where the hypnotized subject is unaware of the instructions that control his or her behavior. Not only did Charcot show the difference between physical and hysterical paralyses; he also managed to create hysterical paralysis in subjects under hypnosis. Charcot was demonstrating that hysterical illnesses have a psychological, not a physical basis; that ultimately these artificial seizures and other bizarre symptoms began not in the body but in the mind.

Freud arrived in Paris like a pauper at a king's court. He was a young medical student, an Austrian who was uncomfortable speaking French, a Jew in a world of Gentiles, and a young man completely separated from his family and friends for the first time in his life. Charcot, on the other hand, was the most famous doctor in all of France, second only to Louis Pasteur, the discoverer of the rabies vaccine and the inventor of pasteurization, a method of eliminating harmful organisms from milk and other foods. Through sheer force of will, assisted by a talent for politics and his wealthy wife, Charcot had built the Salpêtrière Hospital into one of the most prestigious schools in France. Virtually every prominent neurologist in France at that time studied there. Charcot's weekly demonstrations of patients' hysterias and his lectures on neurology were attended by large, spell-bound audiences. Freud described his first impression in a letter to Martha Bernays:

> M. Charcot came in at ten o'clock, a tall man of fifty-eight, a silk hat on his head, with dark and curiously mild eyes (one of them is expressionless and has an inward cast), with long hair held back by his ears, clean shaven, with very expressive features and full protruding lips: in short, like a worldly priest, of whom one expects much wit and that he understands how to live well.

Charcot entertained artists, healed heads of state, and ruled his hospital from a distance, seldom spending time on the wards or with his students. In 1885, he was regularly demonstrating to visitors the "three stages of hysteria" that he had "discovered" in various patients. Unfortunately, Charcot's aloofness left him unaware that his intelligent, suggestible patients had often been trained to demonstrate the "three stages of hysteria" by incompetent hypnotists working on the hospital wards, who had helped them to develop the illness instead of curing it.

Freud wrote to Bernays when he first arrived, "I believe I am changing a great deal. Charcot, who is both one of the greatest of physicians and a man whose common sense is the order of genius, simply demolishes my views and aims. . . . What I certainly know is that no other human being has ever affected me in such a way." Freud admired Charcot's unyielding demand for physical proof for the causes and mechanisms of illness. During one medical lecture, Freud liked to recall, some student contradicted the great master, stating, "But that can't be true, it contradicts the Young-Helmholtz theory." Charcot replied, "Theory is good, but it doesn't prevent things from existing." Freud took this as his motto. Unfortunately, so did Charcot, who never seriously tried to explain how his hypnosis worked.

Freud came to Charcot's laboratory to study anatomical changes in the brains of paralyzed children. He intended to perform dissections under a microscope. Within six weeks of arriving, though, Freud had abandoned the project. He had realized that he was not yet part of Charcot's inner circle of favored students and research staff. He was still just another passerby who did not even merit invitations to Charcot's social gatherings. Discouraged and ignored, Freud was on the verge of leaving Paris for Berlin at the beginning of December. Then he made one more attempt to join Charcot's inner circle. In a letter composed in perfect French by a fluent friend, Freud offered to translate Charcot's third volume of lectures on the nervous system into German. Charcot accepted, and Freud began his true work at Salpêtrière—becoming Charcot's student.

By the time Freud finally left Paris on February 28, 1886, he had been fully adopted into Charcot's clan. He had visited the Charcots' lavish, antique-filled home several times and attended three of their parties. Though he did not enjoy attending these parties, he did enjoy being invited to them. Freud referred to Charcot in his later writings as one of his great teachers, perhaps because so much of Freud's own work builds on Charcot's ideas.

Charcot's hospital, the Salpêtrière, was one of the most prestigious medical institutions in all of France.

In Paris, Freud made several observations. Hysteria was not caused solely by sexual deprivation. Hysteria was a syndrome that could be influenced by the patients' mental experiences. Hypnotism and hysteria seemed to be linked by some hidden mechanism, which the patient could not detect. This last point was crucial to Freud's later work. Hysterical patients had more than one state of consciousness; they would perform commands given to them while they were in a trance *after* they had left the hypnotic state. As Freud later wrote, "I received the profoundest impression of the possibility that there could be powerful mental processes which nevertheless remained hidden from the consciousness of men."

Because hysteria involved physical symptoms caused by a psychological process, Freud wondered how the brain could act to cause the body so much damage. During his time in Paris, a debate raged about whether hysteria was an inherited disease that would only occur in "susceptible" people, or whether it was acquired, like a common cold. The same question could be applied to susceptibility to hypnotic suggestion. Freud was not sure about his own opinion and waffled for years on the matter. Charcot believed that the tendency toward hysteria was hereditary and was activated by a trauma that shocked the nervous system. That idea led Freud to ask several questions about the relationship between physical and mental states. How did psychological trauma transform itself into physical illness? How could a person become ill from a memory? How could hysteria begin?

After returning to Vienna, Freud began to think about unconscious processes, the effect of mental experience on physical symptoms, and the interaction of sexual urges, hysteria, and mental life. He continued to contemplate these issues for the next 50 years. After Freud left Charcot's laboratory, he never performed any experimental work again. His experience at Charcot's laboratory marked the beginning of Freud's career as a clinician.

THE RISE AND FALL OF HYPNOSIS

Hypnosis was extremely unpopular when Charcot revived it as a treatment for hysteria in the 1880s. A century earlier, the German physician Franz Anton Mesmer had popularized a theory of "animal magnetism," which stated that disease was caused by a bad distribution of a magnetic fluid in the body. This fluid was supposed to connect humanity, the earth, and the stars. Mesmer built jars called *baquets* to collect the fluid for his followers. Hypnosis could redistribute this fluid and heal the patient. Mesmer would sit in front of a patient, stare straight into her eyes, pass his hands in front of the patient's face, and then touch the part of the body that was afflicted. Many patients would feel strange sensations or faint when Mesmer touched them; many claimed to be cured. Mesmer's followers refined his technique and put their patients into a "magnetic sleep," or trance. During magnetic sleep, the patients could remember their lives perfectly and could diagnose their maladies. When they awoke, though, they remembered nothing of the trance. Mesmer's followers published textbooks on producing magnetic sleep and healing.

Although Mesmer's movement attracted thousands of followers and spread throughout Europe and to the United States, it was doomed by its oddity. Physicians despised mesmerism, as the new treatment was called, and pointed out that the theory of "animal magnetism" had no basis in fact. The hypnotists would point to occasional extraordinary cures as "proof" that their doctrine was true, instead of analyzing what happened to the rest of their patients, who might undergo dozens of unsuccessful, expensive hypnotic sessions. Moreover, hypnotizing uneducated laymen and having them diagnose their own diseases and prescribe treatment was an illegal medical practice. In 1784, a French royal commission investigated Mesmer's cures and found that they were completely ineffective. The final blow against Mesmer's credibility may have been struck by the many stage hypnotists who demonstrated mesmerism as entertainment rather than a medical treatment. With scientific rationalism coming into fashion, mesmerism lost its charm, and by the 1850s it had largely disappeared.

Toward the end of the 18th century the use of hypnosis to cure disease spread throughout Europe and the United States. However, the practice quickly fell out of favor after several scientific commissions found no medical value in it.

Conversations

Freud was more than ready to abandon the laboratory when he returned to Austria in April 1886. He had spent years investigating eels' organs, gold chloride, cocaine, hemorrhages, and children's brains. After his visit to Charcot's realm, Freud wrote medical research papers only about clinical studies, probing cases of neurological diseases like cerebral palsy and aphasia.

After spending a month studying childhood diseases in Berlin, Freud came back to Vienna to take a job as director of the neurological section at a private clinic for children. He became an expert on childhood cerebral palsy, publishing papers on the topic through 1897. He resigned from the Vienna General Hospital, where he had done his training, to start his own practice (and make more money as well). On Easter Sunday, 1886, he published a newspaper notice that stated, "Dr. Sigmund Freud, Docent for Nervous Diseases at the University, has returned from his study trip to Paris and Berlin and has consulting hours at Rathausstrasse No. 7, from 1 to 2:30."

While Freud was obviously qualified to diagnose and treat children's neurological disorders, he was taking a risk

Freud and Martha Bernays in 1885, the year before their marriage.

by advertising his private practice. Freud was an unknown. He was also working outside of a hospital setting for the first time. Now Freud's adult patients were entirely dependent on him and him alone; there was no community of doctors reviewing and discussing his decisions outside of the children's clinic. Freud was understandably nervous and doubtful about his ability. His old friend Josef Breuer and his former teacher Hermann Nothnagel referred their patients to him, but the work was not steady at first. At one point, Freud considered emigrating to America, but he dropped the idea when a friend informed him that the only work he would find in New York would be waiting on tables.

Soon, though, Freud had a very good reason to stay in Vienna. Sympathetic relatives and a few wealthy friends managed to donate enough money so that Freud could finally marry Martha after an engagement of more than four years. The wedding took place on September 14, 1886. A little over a year later, Martha gave birth to the Freuds' first daughter. The child was named Matilde, after Breuer's wife.

The name Matilde had not been chosen lightly. In 1886, Josef Breuer was one of Freud's closest friends and scientific collaborators. Breuer began his career as a neurological researcher, and before starting his medical practice he made important discoveries concerning regulation of breathing and the inner ear's role in maintaining balance. Freud met Breuer while both men were working in Brücke's laboratory. The two had much in common. Aside from their mutual interest in neurology, Breuer attracted Freud through his cultural and literary interests. Breuer corresponded with Freud's favorite teacher, Franz Brentano, and befriended poets, writers, and composers. He was popular with his colleagues because of his lack of pretension, his sincere interest in philosophy and the arts, and his generosity.

Freud was frequently short of funds, and Breuer regularly loaned him money. In Breuer, Freud once again had a father—not a restrictive authoritarian like Brücke, but

Matilde Freud, the oldest of the Freuds' six children, was named after the wife of one of Freud's closest friends and collaborators, Josef Breuer.

a father nonetheless. In the early years of their friendship, Breuer encouraged Freud's research and referred patients to him.

By the mid-1880s, Breuer, like Freud, was devoting himself full-time to clinical practice. Unlike Freud, however, Breuer was renowned for his clinical talent and treated some of the wealthiest families in Vienna, as well as the poorest. Breuer also treated one of Freud's most famous "patients," Anna O.

When he was not taking time off for army service or his honeymoon, Freud worked on Charcot's behalf. Publicly, he served his great teacher by giving a lecture to the Society of Physicians on October 15, 1886. Freud had intended to introduce the idea of male hysteria to the Viennese medical community and discuss classifications of hysteria. Unfortunately, the Viennese were already aware of male hysteria. One physician in the audience noted that he had published studies of male hysteria 16 years earlier. Several of the professors present objected angrily that Freud was presenting a matter of common knowledge instead of new research.

Freud took this rejection to heart. He felt that he was being persecuted for discussing male hysteria. There is no evidence that the Society of Physicians was unusually cruel to Freud or that they disapproved of anything aside from the fact that his paper was not original. But Freud, still smarting from the cocaine episode, felt isolated and attacked. A month after his first lecture to the Society of Physicians he gave a second lecture, exhibiting a victim of male hysteria; after that, he did not return to the society for the rest of his 52 years' residence in Vienna.

While he was struggling for recognition, Freud was seeing patients. Frequently, these patients suffered from hysteria. They did not display learned seizures or complain that half of their body was paralyzed, like Charcot's hysterics. They were not hospitalized, and their symptoms were more subtle. Strange pains, nausea, facial tics, single-limb paralyses, perceiving unpleasant odors, and attacks of dizziness were among the symptoms they reported. By definition, there was no known physical cause for these patients' distress, and their disorders sometimes clashed with known facts about the course of disease and the structure of the body. Freud, like other 19th-century neurologists, used many methods to treat hysteria. He prescribed massage, electric shock, baths, and the Weir Mitchell rest cure, which required bed rest in isolation and a spoon-fed diet of soft, milky food in addition to massage and mild electric shock. However, as he continued his practice, Freud became convinced that hypnotism was the best possible treatment for these patients.

text continues on page 48

STRONG MEDICINE

When Freud began his practice, he used therapies that seem odd to modern doctors. One treatment was faradization, a sort of electrical therapy. Patients would take off their clothes, sit in a chair, and put their bare feet in a basin of water connected to one pole of a magnetic coil. The doctor held an electrode in his hand, allowing him to pass electrical current through the patient's body. When the patient was shocked, her muscles would contract, causing trembling, nausea, dizziness, and fainting. She would also suffer electrical burns that left red marks. Another popular cure was hydrotherapy. Patients were sprayed with strong jets of cold water in spurts or wrapped in cold wet sheets and rubbed until they became warm. The force of the water and the rubbing were both supposed to be important for good health.

Freud's mentor, Jean-Martin Charcot, devised this vibrating hat driven by an electric motor in an attempt to treat some neurological disorders.

text continued from page 46

Freud began to use hypnosis to treat hysteria while he was still bedazzled by Charcot. He had seen Charcot controlling hysterical patients through hypnotic suggestion by simply telling them what to do while they were in a trance. Yet Charcot had never used hypnosis to *cure* hysterical symptoms. On one occasion, a visitor to the Salpêtrière asked one of Charcot's assistants what the use of hypnotism was, if it was not being used to cure patients. The assistant replied that "the hypnotized hysterical woman is to be regarded as the 'psychological frog,' and that what the frog had done for physiology, the hysterical woman is to do for psychology." In this view, hypnosis was simply a way to display specimens for study.

Charcot's hypnotic technique was simple. He would stare into his patients' eyes, and they would fall into a trance. Freud tried this technique but began to have doubts within his first year of practice. Some of his patients were "unhypnotizable." Others did not respond to suggestion at all. Freud described his method of hypnotizing patients in "A Case of Successful Treatment by Hypnotism," published in two parts in 1892–93. His patient was unable to breast-feed her second baby.

> I at once attempted to induce hypnosis by ocular [eye] fixation, at the same time making constant suggestions of the symptoms of sleep. After three minutes the patient was lying back with the peaceful expression of someone in profound sleep. . . . I made use of suggestion to contradict all her fears and the feelings on which those fears were based: "Have no fear! You will make an excellent nurse and the baby will thrive." The patient went on sleeping while I left her for a few minutes, and when I had woken her up showed amnesia for what had occurred. Before I left the house I was also under the necessity of contradicting a worried remark by the patient's husband to the effect that a woman's nerves might be totally ruined by hypnosis.

Hypnotism was a controversial treatment. Charcot had rescued the technique from obscurity and ill repute, but physicians were still leery of this frankly nonmedical technique. Neither Charcot nor any other researcher had established a physical or biological reason why hypnotism should work. One of Freud's former teachers, Theodor Meynert, objected that hypnotism made patients mere helpless animals and that all hypnotic cures were fakes or delusions. He worried that hypnotism could only make hysteric patients worse, a possibility that worried Charcot as well. Perhaps most prophetically, Meynert stated that hypnosis worked by turning off a part of the brain that produced "higher cortical activity" (conscious thought), leaving only the "subcortex" (thought to be the source of animal desires) to control behavior. According to Meynert, this shutdown would unleash the subcortex's sexual urges, obviously a horrifying idea. Both Charcot and Meynert believed that hypnotism worked through a biological energy, that some part of the body was physically changed by the process of hypnotism.

Not everyone agreed with this view. In 1887, Freud began to translate a book on "suggestion" by the French

This painting shows Charcot giving a demonstration of the powers of hypnosis to a large group of admirers. Freud hung a reproduction of this work in his office.

physician Hippolyte Bernheim, a recognized expert on hypnotism. Bernheim believed that the uncanny effects of hypnosis were due to psychological suggestion. More shockingly, Bernheim claimed that the ability to be hypnotized was not limited to hysterics. According to Bernheim, everyone could be hypnotized, even without the inherited tendency toward illness that doctors then believed existed in hysteric patients.

Freud opted for an explanation that included both physical and psychological processes. He saw mental activity as dependent on physiological states but not identical with them. This is a subtle point, and it is important for understanding Freud's later theories of hysteria and other mental illnesses. Think of a person who is awakened at night by a loud noise. That person will be startled; her heart will pound, she will sweat, and she will sit up in bed suddenly. But that person's mental reaction will depend on her prior experience. Someone who lives in a neighborhood where crime and guns are common may become frightened, paralyzed with fear. Another person, who does not like being awakened at night, may simply become angry and jump out of bed to investigate the source of the noise. In these cases, the physical stimulus and the initial physical reaction are the same, but the emotional state that follows is very different.

In short, when Freud considered hypnotism, he understood that he was dealing with the mind–body problem. As a trained neurologist, he was constantly confronted with questions about where the body ended and where the mind began, about how thought affected the body, and how thoughts came to be in the first place.

In 1880, Freud's friend Josef Breuer had begun to see a patient he called Anna O. This young woman, whose real name was Bertha Pappenheim, was 21 years old when she fell ill. She was a member of a wealthy Jewish family, cultured and intelligent, fluent in English, and a reader of French and Italian literature. Yet Breuer wrote that she lived a "monotonous life, restricted to her family." At the time of her symptoms' onset, she had just spent several months nursing her sick father.

Anna O. came to Breuer complaining of headaches, numbness, paralysis, and various visual problems. Over the next year, she also began to have hallucinations in which she saw snakes and skeletons, and she lost the ability to speak German (she continued to communicate in English and French). At times, she seemed to switch between two personalities: one sad, but otherwise normal; the other anxious, rude, and prone to hallucinations. These personalities became more distinct over time. By December 1881, Breuer discovered that he could make Anna O. shift into the unhealthy personality by showing her an orange (oranges were virtually all that Anna ate during the first part of her illness). This second personality seemed to be living exactly one year earlier in time from the "healthy" personality, which Breuer confirmed by looking at her mother's diary of Anna's illness.

Clearly, Anna O. was not a typical hysteric. She did respond to hypnosis, but not in the usual way. In the evenings, Anna O. would spontaneously enter a hypnotic state and tell Breuer things about her hallucinations that she could not remember at other times. Reporting her miserable fantasies relieved Anna O., and her symptoms would disappear for the night. Anna O. called this her "talking cure." For example, one spring day in 1882, Anna O. stopped drinking any liquids. She became more and more dehydrated, until one night, while under hypnosis, she told Breuer that she had become disgusted when she saw a dog lap water out of a glass. Once she had told Breuer this story, she was able to drink again.

Bertha Pappenheim, complaining of headaches, paralysis, and other problems, went to see Freud's colleague Josef Breuer. In an effort to protect her anonymity, he referred to her in his discussions with other doctors as "Anna O." Under Breuer's care, she became the first patient to undergo psychoanalysis.

Following this pattern, Breuer helped Anna O. banish all her symptoms by having her recall how each one began. Most of the symptoms arose when Anna O. had to suppress some emotion. This was a long, tedious treatment; Anna recounted 303 different instances of symptoms involving her hearing alone. But the simple act of acknowledging her feelings seemed to cure her—if she remembered them in exact reverse chronological order. And yet all her remembering occurred when she was in a state of self-hypnosis. Anna O.'s treatment took place when she was in an altered state of consciousness.

It is important to remember that it was Anna O., not Breuer, who first suggested this treatment, which she called "the talking cure." Breuer simply encouraged Anna in her approach. Anna O. most likely got the idea from a popular book on catharsis that had been published in 1880. The author was Jacob Bernays, Martha Freud's uncle. In addition, Aristotle's concept of dramatic catharsis—he maintained that tragic dramas allow audience members to release their own violent emotions safely—was very popular in Viennese salons at the time. Anna O. was putting on her own play to release her own emotions. She chose both the method of the "talking cure" and the timing of her treatment, which she began about a year after her father finally died in the spring of 1881. She was like Mesmer's hypnotized patients, who would diagnose their own disorders.

Anna O. and Breuer did eventually manage to list all the numerous sources of her troubles. She was temporarily cured. However, within three months of her last session with Breuer, she was institutionalized in a sanitarium. Once again, she was unable to speak German, suffered lapses of memory, and had severe headaches. Five years later, she still suffered from occasional hallucinations.

Anna O.'s therapy became extremely important to Freud's theories of mental illness. He believed (as he expressed it in a paper on hysteria he later wrote with

Breuer) that "hysterics suffer mainly from reminiscences." If the disturbing memories could be recalled, all would be well. If a patient could only find the source of his or her problem, he believed, that problem would disappear. In other words, the truth will set you free. Unfortunately, not all patients could remember the "truth" as easily as Anna O. did.

Anna O., or Bertha Pappenheim, went on to become a philanthropist, social activist, and writer. She directed an orphanage, founded the League of Jewish Women, and traveled through the Near East and eastern Europe to help orphans and investigate forced prostitution. In 1954, West Germany issued a postage stamp in her honor. Perhaps her greatest contribution to the world, though, was simply instructing Breuer to serve as her doctor and confidant. Breuer titled his therapeutic process the "cathartic method."

While Breuer listened to Anna O.'s recollections, he was also consulting with his good friend Sigmund Freud over dinner. The case excited Freud. He tried to tell Charcot about Anna O., but Charcot was not interested in cases outside his own hospital. Freud was eager to publish a description of Anna O.'s symptoms and treatment, but Breuer was reluctant, and the case study was not published until 1895. Breuer felt, correctly, that the case was not typical of hysteria. Soon, Breuer and Freud also came to disagree about the meaning of Anna O.'s symptoms and Breuer's treatment of her. Freud saw sexual elements in Anna's case that Breuer could not defend.

By the mid-1880s, Freud needed a new friend and confidant, someone who wished to explore the mind in depth and who was willing to listen patiently to Freud's most bizarre, innovative ideas. Freud found his perfect companion in Breuer's friend Wilhelm Fliess.

4

Explanations

Wilhelm Fliess, an ear, nose, and throat specialist from Berlin, was a man of strong, odd opinions. Today, most of his ideas sound like hoaxes, but in the late 19th century, they were no more nor less suspicious than Freud's theories. Freud, after all, was intrigued by the scientifically muddy topic of telepathy (psychic communication) and published three papers on it during his lifetime.

Fliess is known for stating three main theories: human bisexuality, human periodicity, and the nasal-genital theory. According to Fliess, humans contain the physical and psychological characteristics of both sexes, starting from conception in the womb. In his view, each sex was supposed have a separate and distinct sexual cycle, or periodicity. This "vital periodicity," as Fliess called it, not only governed sexual functions such as ovulation and menstruation but also controlled phenomena like migraine headaches and nosebleeds. The woman's cycle, Fliess reasoned, was 28 days long—the approximate length of the menstrual cycle, and a man's cycle lasted 23 days. Finally, Fliess believed that all humans shared a connection between specific locations in the nose and the genital organs:

Freud (right) with his friend and colleague, Wilhelm Fliess. The two shared an interest in revolutionary theories of human sexuality.

an injury to a nasal membrane would affect a particular genital region.

Each of these theories had a basis in sound scientific data, and each had its pitfalls. Many animals, including humans, show features of both sexes' genitals during development in the womb. Fliess also knew of certain crustaceans (a class of invertebrate animals that includes shrimp and crabs) that changed sex over the course of their lives, and he was familiar with a famous case of a woman who seemed to change sex in her early 30s. There are also several established similarities between the nose and the genitals. For example, some nasal tissues swell during a woman's menstrual period, and some people suffer nosebleeds or sneezing attacks when they are intensely excited sexually. However, Fliess believed in a direct, almost mystical link between the nose and the genitals. Fliess's faith in his ideas later led Freud to make a disastrous error in caring for one of his own patients.

Similarly, Fliess had many interesting and complex methods for deriving the 28- and 23-day human cycles, based on the timing of childbirth and menstruation, the development of human embryos, and miscarriage rates. Again, this was not such a strange idea at the time. Dozens of scientists were searching for a mathematical key to life—exploring the differences in gestation periods (the time from conception to birth or hatching) between species, the duration of various diseases, and other phenomena.

Unfortunately, according to *Scientific American* columnist Martin Gardner, since Fliess chose two numbers, 23 and 28, that do not share any common factors (that is, they are not divisible by the same number), he could manipulate the formula $X \times 23$ (+ or -) $Y \times 28$ to generate any number he pleased. Fliess did so and calculated anything from life spans to the onset of menstruation to death dates. Until his 52nd birthday, Freud fearfully believed that he would die at age 51 (23 + 28).

All of Fliess's major beliefs have been scientifically discredited, but when Freud first met Fliess, these ideas seemed exciting and grand. After all, Fliess was interested in the same issues as Freud: life, death, and sex. Fliess was very well-read in both medicine and research biology, which is one reason why he was able to defend his theories so successfully. Freud considered him his intellectual superior when they first met, and he eagerly sought his friend's advice on all his work.

Freud and Fliess started corresponding shortly after meeting in 1887. In the years from 1894 to 1900, Fliess exerted a profound influence on Freud. Freud discussed with Fliess every idea he conceived, through letters and daylong discussions during shared vacations. Freud told Fliess, "Your praise is nectar and ambrosia to me." "When I talked to you," he went on, "and saw that you thought something of me, I actually started thinking something of myself." (In Freud's own home, his work "stopped at the nursery door," as he put it, and there is no evidence that Martha Freud discussed her husband's work with him.) Freud wrote to Fliess about his patients, his theories on hysteria and art, his children's growth and illnesses, and everything else that occupied his mind and heart. For many years, Fliess was Freud's best friend.

In 1888, though, Freud was more concerned with his patients than with Fliess. Freud had begun to use Anna O.'s cathartic technique in his practice, but certain patients could not be hypnotized. In 1889, Freud brought a patient who seemed to be a good candidate for cathartic treatment to visit Hippolyte Bernheim, the hypnotism expert in France, for advice. This patient, Emmy von N. (Baroness Fanny Moser), was a well-off middle-aged widow who had begun to show hysterical symptoms 14 years earlier, when her husband died. Freud treated her for about 15 weeks. She suffered from loss of appetite, convulsive tics of her face and neck, a stammer, and hallucinations of slithering snakes and dead rats.

Bernheim showed Freud that patients who had been hypnotized could be made to remember things in their later waking state that they could not describe before. When the patient awoke, Bernheim would tell her to remember, while putting pressure on the patient's forehead with his hand. Freud concluded that all patients knew the source of their hysterical symptoms, even the patients who could not be hypnotized. The problem was to tap those memories without hypnosis. Freud used the "pressure" technique for a few years after he returned to Vienna.

Yet "pressure" did not cure Emmy von N. One day, when Freud questioned her about an interesting event she had mentioned, Emmy Von N. became angry, and insisted, Freud later recalled in *Studies on Hysteria* (written with Breuer), that Freud stop "asking her where this or that came from, but let her tell what she had to say." Freud relented, and he let Emmy von N. continue in what was to become the first instance of another psychoanalytic technique: free association. He did not try to interrupt her talking. Instead, he sat by while Emmy von N. spoke about whatever she liked, for as long as she liked.

Another patient, Elisabeth von R., would talk for a while and then fall silent. Freud refused to accept the idea that there was nothing left in her head. Like Anna O., Freud thought, she was suffering because she had forgotten what caused her symptoms. Freud pressed her to keep talking, even when she thought her mind was empty.

Emmy von N. and Elisabeth von R. were helped by their treatment, but it was not clear to Freud why it worked. At the time that Freud was treating Emmy von N., he was still seeking common features between hysterical states and hypnotism. Freud and Breuer, like Charcot, were interested in the mechanism of hysteria, the way in which emotional problems were transformed into physical symptoms.

In the late 1880s, Freud began to see a source, if not a mechanism, for hysteria. He began to believe that the cause

Freud's treatment of Baroness Fanny Moser (referred to by Freud as "Emmy von N.") marked the beginning of the use of "free association"—letting the patient talk about whatever comes into his or her head.

of hysteria was sexual repression. Charcot and Breuer had both hinted to Freud that most hysterical problems began in "the marriage bed," and Freud himself had witnessed demonstrations of the erotic nature of therapy. When Freud was still using hypnosis, an easily hypnotized female subject once threw her arms around his neck upon awakening from a trance. Freud was saved from this embarrassing entanglement when a servant entered, but he never used hypnosis with that patient again.

Freud also saw clues to the source of hysteria in Breuer's final session with Anna O., which took place in 1882. After Breuer and Anna O. had finally banished her last symptom, Breuer left Anna O.'s house. He returned that evening to find her bent over with pain from severe abdominal cramps. When Breuer asked Anna O. what was wrong, she replied "Now Dr. B.'s child is coming!" Anna O. was suffering from a hysterical pregnancy and simulated birth pangs. Horrified, Breuer hypnotized her, fled the house, and left Vienna the next day for a vacation with his wife.

Neither Freud nor Breuer believed that Anna O.'s illnesses were caused by sexual repression—at first. Yet Anna O.'s symptoms revealed that she felt a sexual bond between herself and her doctor, much like Freud's hypnotized patient. In another case, when Freud performed a medical examination on Elisabeth von R., she swooned when he pressed her thigh. According to Freud, she "assumed a peculiar expression, one of pleasure rather than of pain; she cried out . . . her face flushed, she threw back her head, closed her eyes, her trunk bent backward." Freud and Breuer were arousing sexual urges in their hysterical patients.

Freud and Breuer published a short paper titled "On the Psychical Mechanism of Hysterical Phenomena: Preliminary Communication," in 1893, and the book *Studies on Hysteria* in 1895, but they had discussed most of their findings for years beforehand. In *Studies* and the "Communication," Freud and Breuer unveiled a new, psychologically based theory of hysteria.

"Hysterics suffer mainly from reminiscences," wrote Breuer and Freud in the "Communication." In their publications, Freud and Breuer established that hysteria is the result of a psychic trauma, not a physical injury. Yet they assumed that there was a sort of force or energy that was transformed in the course of hysteria. Freud and Breuer believed that this energy was like electricity. The human brain, they wrote, tries to maintain a constant, low energy state. Pain and anguish is the result of a buildup of this energy; its discharge caused pleasure. Over time, Freud would gradually shape these ideas into a general theory of neuroses, or mental illnesses that seem to involve anxiety.

Freud and Breuer's theory of the development of hysteria can be summarized as follows: In the course of a trauma, a great deal of mental energy is created. Somehow, the trauma is removed from consciousness, whether because the subject was in a state of self-hypnosis or because the incident was too painful to keep in consciousness. Yet the energy built up by trauma stays in the body. As the trauma fades from consciousness, this energy flows to the body, causing physical symptoms. When the patient is hypnotized in a clinic, though, the patient can remember the trauma and can be cured of the hysterical symptoms by discharging its energy into words in the presence of the doctor.

Freud did not specify exactly what this "energy" might be. This was not an uncommon practice at the time. Several other scientists writing on how physical stimuli affected human sensations and judgment (a topic called psychophysics) referred to the "forces" of the mind. But readers should not confuse this metaphor with a scientific explanation. Freud did not prove that there were sources of energy in the head or show exactly what it was that changed when a person became hysterical. Freud relied on his previous biological training to tell him what sorts of ideas might be appropriate for explaining how painful thought became a physical illness.

In fact, Freud's methods cannot be called conventionally scientific at all. Freud did not carry out controlled experiments on his patients. He never randomly varied his approach to them, to see what effect he might have on them. He also never limited himself to observing his wealthy, ailing patients to chart the natural course of their illnesses. Instead, Freud tried to help them.

This is the strength, and weakness, of Freud's techniques. Freud relied on his patients for new insights and confirmations of his theories. He was a keen observer, but what did he have to observe? Freud did not witness his patients' symptoms, but rather his own interaction with those symptoms. As Anna O. had shown, a therapist can have a powerful effect on a patient's mental life, and not necessarily a good one.

Freud presented his observations in the form of case studies. In the course of a case study, Freud would write a chronological summary of the patient's illness, from the first symptoms to the patient's state at the end of treatment. Unfortunately, to protect his patients' privacy, Freud changed many of the facts in his cases. This censorship, though kind, sometimes distorted his research. In the case of Katharina R., one of the patients described in *Studies*, Freud changed the identity of a man who attempted to seduce his patient from her father to an uncle. This sometimes made it difficult for others reviewing his work to make their own judgments about the patient's problems.

Similarly, because the case studies were records of individual therapy, no one else could try to reproduce them. In most sciences, researchers duplicate published experiments to see if they work. Reproducing the results helps to show that the original researchers described their procedures accurately and that the results were not a fluke. Freud's case studies, by definition, are portrayals of specific people, and they cannot be reproduced. However, other researchers could try to use Freud's procedures on their own patients, or reanalyze what he had written.

Freud also had a professional reputation to maintain, so many of his cases were presented as examples of successful therapy, even when the patient ended treatment with mixed results, as Anna O. did. When Freud's patients were not fully cured by his methods, he had very little motivation to publicize their suffering. Essentially, Freud's fellow practi-

text continues on page 64

"I made an excursion . . . so that for a while I might forget medicine and more particularly the neuroses," wrote Freud in *Studies on Hysteria* (1895). Freud was vacationing in the mountains when 18-year-old Katharina, who worked at the inn, asked him about her symptoms. She was dizzy, short of breath, and felt like she would suffocate, all classical hysterical symptoms. He told her, "You must have seen or heard something that very much embarrassed you, and that you'd much rather not have seen."

Katharina told Freud that two years before she had seen her father lying on top of her cousin Barbara. At that point, Katharina said, "Everything went blank, my eyelids were forced together and there was a hammering and buzzing in my head."

Two days later, Katharina fell ill. Freud thought that she was sick from disgust—but at what? After further questioning, Katharina reported that her father "had made sexual advances to her herself, when she was only fourteen years old," when she "woke up suddenly 'feeling his body' in the bed." Katharina, annoyed at being awakened, did not recognize that she was being attacked sexually until she saw her cousin and her father together.

Freud wrote, "She had not been disgusted by the sight of the two people but by the memory which that sight had stirred up in her." When Katharina remembered what had happened, "the sulky unhappy face had grown lively, her eyes were bright, she was lightened and exalted." She was cured.

text continued from page 62

tioners had to accept his case studies on faith. They had to trust that any information Freud left out was irrelevant, that he left enough of the remaining material intact to make sense out of the case, and that he would not cling to old methods in the face of unsuccessful therapy.

At the same time, Freud's case studies were extremely valuable. Though the case studies always described individuals, Freud was careful to show how each patient illustrated universal aspects of his theories. The particular case could be fit into a category of illness, a pattern of mental functioning. Obviously, case studies gave Freud's audience a chance to see exactly how he used his theories in actual clinical practice. Freud's case studies gave his readers a chance to see how his theories applied to real, dysfunctional people.

Freud genuinely believed that his hysterical patients needed only to be freed from repressed memories to be cured of their symptoms. In his case studies, he showed how a therapist could make this happen. The studies enabled Freud to show his audience exactly how he figured out his patients' secrets. More than one author has compared Freud's case studies to detective novels, where the doctor deduces the source of the patient's troubles from a few murky, subtle clues. At each stage of treatment, the reader could see if he agreed with Freud's deductions. The full implications of Freud's reasoning were available for all to see.

Whatever the potential flaws of Freud's method, he was passionate about his research. Freud wrote to Fliess in 1895, "A man like me cannot live without a hobby horse, without a dominating passion, without—to speak with Schiller—a tyrant, and he has come my way. And in his service I now know no moderation. It is psychology." Finally, with his new revelations, he might have a chance at the fame denied him in the past.

In 1896, Freud felt the need of a new term to describe his work. He had stopped using hypnosis and suggestion, and was conducting therapy using free association as his major method of treatment. To emphasize his study of the mind, Freud at first used the term "psychological analysis," introduced by the French physician and researcher Pierre Janet. But by 1896, Freud's therapy was based on his own work, not Janet's. Freud decided to call his approach psychoanalysis.

Freud (far right) with his two sisters and their children on a summer vacation in 1900. Each summer the Freuds would leave Vienna for a vacation in the mountains.

Departures

By the 1890s, Freud was becoming an established physician and a thoroughly proper member of the middle class. In 1891, the Freuds moved to Berggasse 19. Freud lived in that building for the next 47 years, until he fled from the Nazis in 1938. The Freuds filled their household with rugs, tables, glasses, servants—and children. After their daughter Matilde was born in 1887, the Freud family rapidly expanded, with Jean Martin (called Martin by his family) arriving in 1889, followed by Oliver (1891), Ernst (1892), Sophie (1893), and Anna (1895). Freud had a habit of naming his children after his own friends and mentors, not Martha's; Jean Martin was named for Charcot; Oliver for Oliver Cromwell, the 17th-century British revolutionary who overthrew the monarchy; Ernst for Brücke; Matilde for Breuer's wife; Sophie and Anna after the daughter and niece of a high school teacher.

Martha Freud nursed the children through diphtheria, colds, chicken pox, and flu and ensured that the midday meal was served promptly each day. Freud particularly enjoyed boiled beef, and he disliked poultry; "One should not kill chickens," he would tell his children. "Let them stay alive and lay eggs."

From autumn through spring, Freud worked six days a week. He saw patients from 8:00 to 12:00, wrote up notes, ate at 1:00, took a walk, then spoke with other doctors or saw more patients from 3:00 until 9:00. Freud's son Martin remembered occasions when his father worked 16 to 18 hours a day. On Saturday he played cards with old friends, including Dr. Leopold Königstein, who had researched cocaine with him, and on Sundays he visited his mother. As for holidays, Martin Freud later remembered, "Our festivals were Christmas, with presents under a candle-lit tree, and Easter, with gaily painted Easter eggs. I had never been to a synagogue, nor to my knowledge had my brothers or sisters."

Each year, the Freuds would leave Vienna in May or June and go to a resort in the mountains. Martha and the children would leave first, along with Martha's sister Minna, who joined the household in the 1890s after her fiancé died of tuberculosis. Freud would generally keep working through July, then join the family for a holiday through the middle of September. He would often spend a few weeks travelling on his own, though, to view ancient ruins and archeological sites. The children would daily tramp up and down the Bavarian hills, looking for strawberries. In late summer, Freud would lead his brood on mushroom hunts, teaching them to identify poisonous toadstools and to fearlessly devour choice specimens.

Freud loved his children, though at the beginning of his marriage he did not plan to have six. Both Sigmund and Martha hoped that her last pregnancy, with Anna, was an early menopause. Freud was deeply concerned about his children's health and wrote to Fliess about their every illness—each malady always seemed to travel from child to child until all of them had had their turn. When Matilde almost died after surgery in 1905, he threw a slipper against a wall, breaking one of his favorite marble statuettes. Freud later wrote in *The Psychopathology of Everyday Life*, "My attack of destructive fury served therefore to express a feeling of gratitude to fate and allowed me to perform a '*sacrificial act*'—rather as if I had made a vow to sacrifice something or other as a thank-offering if she recovered her health!"

Despite his many distractions, Freud still found time to contemplate the origin of mental illness. As time went on, Freud became firmly convinced that sexual repression was the root cause of hysteria. In 1894 he wrote, "In all the cases I have analyzed it was the subject's sexual life that had given rise to a distressing affect [emotion]." Freud embraced a sexual theory of hysteria; Breuer shrank from it. Both had their reasons.

Breuer wrote in *Studies on Hysteria* (1895), "The sexual instinct is undoubtedly the most powerful source of persisting increases in excitation (and consequently of neuroses)." In other words, sexual urges bring an increase in the mental "energy" that Freud and Breuer thought had to be "discharged." However, Breuer believed that sex might not be the only source of mental energy. By 1894, Freud had come to believe that frustrated sexual urges were the sole source of hysterical symptoms.

This difference of clinical opinion was the source of the rift between the two men. Breuer was a careful, rigorous researcher; he had delayed publishing his findings about the inner ear until he had confirmed his results in several species. Breuer's perfectionism and self-doubt delayed the publication of Anna O.'s case study for 12 years after he finished her analysis, and he was still uncomfortable with the content. He later wrote, "I confess that the plunging into sexuality in theory and practice is not to my taste." At the same time, researchers in France were also publishing work on hysteria that made Freud and Breuer's work look less original.

Freud, on the other hand, felt pressure to succeed after the cocaine episode and the failure of his paper on male hysteria. Freud fervently believed in his theory and wanted to advertise it as much as possible before someone else stole his ideas. He viewed Breuer's caution as a betrayal. Freud's relationship with Breuer was made even worse by the large debt Freud owed Breuer for sharing Anna O. and the cathartic method of therapy with him, not to mention Breuer's loans at the time of Freud's marriage.

Breuer now appeared to be a holdover from the past, keeping Freud's career back. Freud had battled Breuer to bring *Studies* into print. By the time the book was published in 1895, Freud and Breuer were no longer on good terms. Breuer could not accept sexual energy as the only cause of hysteria, and Freud could not tolerate his doubt. Freud spoke with Breuer less and less, and by 1897 Freud actively avoided his onetime collaborator and friend. Now Freud relied entirely on Wilhelm Fliess for support and criticism of his developing theories.

While Freud was contemplating hysteria, he was also developing therapeutic techniques. Emmy von N., Anna O., and Elizabeth R. had introduced Freud to the "talking cure" and the use of Breuer's cathartic method. He had learned to actively listen to his patients' stories and push them to find the source of their symptoms. Freud was successful enough in his practice that he became ambitious. He began to write a book on the fundamental theory of psychology.

Freud had many goals for the *Project for a Scientific Psychology*. Like almost every psychological researcher who has lived since the Renaissance, Freud wished to demonstrate that there were reliable laws that ruled human behavior. Freud sought to show that these laws could be reduced to the mechanical, chemical, and physical principles that governed all other matter, just as his anti-vitalist professor Ernst Brücke had attempted to do years before. In short, Freud wanted to demonstrate that psychology was simply another specialized science.

Oliver, Martin, and Ernst, Freud's three boys. Freud was a kind and attentive father and often wrote proudly to his colleagues about his children's undertakings.

Yet Freud had other reasons for beginning the *Project*. Freud and Breuer had spent much time explaining the basis of hysteria and mental illness, but they had not managed to explain how a healthy mind operates. Freud also wanted to explore the question of repression. What physical laws govern how the mind protects itself from painful memories?

In the *Project*, Freud described how energy travels through the brain. The brain, he said, receives "excitation," either from events in the outer world or from within the body. Two principles determine how this energy is moved. "Inertia" is the brain's tendency to discharge energy, and "constancy" is the tendency to keep the total amount of excitation in the brain constant. To understand how this energy was controlled, Freud conceived of "structures" of the brain that handled excitation. He called these structures "neurones." Pleasure was the discharge of energy, "unpleasure" the buildup of excitation.

These structures were supposed to perform two different functions, called primary and secondary processes. In the primary process, energy was allowed to flow freely through the brain. In the secondary process, the brain distinguishes between various external and internal stimuli and blocks some of them. This act of "judgment," wrote Freud, is performed by a mental structure known as the *ego*. The ego "binds" energy, stopping hallucinations and other chance occurrences from disturbing the mind.

When he created this complicated theory of mental energy, Freud was not relying on anatomical or biological knowledge of the brain. He was not really talking about physical structures at all. Freud was describing mental *processes* that in some undefined way were supported by the brain's biological functioning. But Freud knew that his conception of the mind was incomplete without a biological or mechanical model of the process of keeping upsetting ideas unconscious, or repression. Descriptions of shifting energies were not enough.

This is one reason why his friendship with Fliess was so very important to Freud. He hoped that Fliess would provide him with the biological foundation he needed to justify his psychological mechanisms. Fliess's collaboration could enable Freud, who was a biologist himself, to contemplate the mind, not the brain. As Freud wrote to Fliess, "The thought that both of us are occupied with the same kind of work is by far the most enjoyable one I can conceive at present. I see how, via the detour of medical practice, you are reaching your first ideal of understanding human beings as a physiologist, just as I most secretly nourish the hope of arriving, via these same paths, at my initial goal of philosophy."

Freud composed a document with several chapters summarizing his ideas and dispatched it to Fliess for his approval on October 8, 1895. Despite his frenzied writing, though, Freud had his doubts. In his letters to Fliess, he veered away from describing his "writing fever" to reporting migraine attacks and fatigue and declared that he was "overworked, irritable and confused." In the end, Freud could not create either a biological or mechanical model of the repression he had set out to explain. Descriptions of shifting energies were not enough, and he finally abandoned the *Project*.

Though Freud's conception of the mind was incomplete at this point, his approach was sound. He had produced an internally logical scheme describing how physical energy is converted into mental energy. Freud's *Project* has been termed "Newtonian" by many writers. Like Isaac Newton's views of the universal laws of motion and gravitation, which were both revolutionary and incomplete, Freud had taken the first steps to put psychology on a scientific basis. He had asserted that the thought content of the mind could produce dysfunctional behavior, that under normal circumstances disturbing thoughts could somehow be censored, and that therefore there were different levels of thought, some of which the conscious mind was not aware of.

Freud also believed as early as 1896 that the root cause of all neurosis or mental illness was sex. Freud divided neuroses into the "psychoneuroses," hysterias and obsessions produced by a childhood sexual trauma, and the "actual neuroses," which were brought on by abnormalities in the patient's adult sex life. Victims of actual neurosis, Freud believed, suffered from sexual frustration, particularly from masturbation and coitus interruptus (withdrawal of the penis from the vagina during intercourse before the male has achieved orgasm).

This simplistic view of adult sexuality—that deprivation of sexual pleasure automatically leads to mental illness—has been dismissed by most modern researchers and therapists. Freud himself later rejected his earlier view. Yet many present-day theorists feel that Freud may have been right in 1896 when he began to assert that some adult neuroses are specifically caused by childhood sexual abuse inflicted by an adult.

Freud's theory of hysteria was a theory of memory. He called it the "seduction theory." In this model, hysterical symptoms are originally caused by a childhood sexual trauma that produces an intense reaction. At the time of the abuse the child cannot fully comprehend what has happened. At puberty, though, the sexually mature hysteric may undergo some minor stress. This new trauma ordinarily would not be severe enough to cause hysteria, but it could revive memories of the childhood sexual abuse, which the young adult can now understand. The childhood trauma transfers its energy to the new experience, and the patient suddenly acquires excess excitation. This energy is discharged in the form of physical symptoms, such as paralysis.

Obsessions were a different matter. When obsessive patients had their childhood sexual experiences, they did not suffer the same way as hysterics. Obsessives felt pleasure. Yet obsessives are not able to convert their excess excitation into physical symptoms. Instead, the obsessive manages to separate the forbidden idea from his excitation. This energy, now free, attaches itself to some other, more acceptable idea, which the mind returns to over and over again. In essence, obsessions are expressions of guilt, whereas hysteria is a memory of abuse. Freud, in his Victorian way, thought that these ideas explained why hysteria was so much more common in women, whereas obsessions were more common in men. He accepted the prevailing notion that women were passive and frightened by sex; men actively enjoyed it. Freud, the great critic of middle-class Victorian culture, could not fully free himself from its prejudices.

The seduction theory was Freud's masterpiece, a synthesis of all his previous work. The seduction theory convincingly explained how hysterical symptoms were produced and why all of his patients' problems seemed to involve sex. On April 21, 1896, Freud gave a lecture to a Viennese psychiatric society on his evolving ideas of the origins of hysteria. He declared that he was like an explorer examining the ruins of an ancient city when he dug through a hysteric's painful past. Each of the 18 cases of hysteria that he had treated, Freud claimed, showed that hysteria originated in childhood sexual abuse. Freud compared this revelation to the discovery of the headwaters of the Nile. Yet Freud reported that when his patients recounted scenes of sexual abuse, they did not feel as though they were remembering them, as they did when they found other mislaid memories.

The reaction to Freud's talk was summed up by Richard von Krafft-Ebing, a respected sex researcher in his own right, who declared, "It sounds like a scientific fairy tale." The sex theory was not the problem; many psychiatric case studies of girls who had been abused by their fathers had already been published. However, most experts believed that hysteria was caused by either purely physical trauma or some inborn tendency to develop the condition, not by an upsetting experience. By 1896, Freud had dispensed with these accepted ideas of hysteria. Though he continued to use biological metaphors in his work, he was now developing a purely psychological theory of mental illness.

The previous year, Freud had witnessed a graphic demonstration of what can happen when a psychological problem is treated as a physical illness. During the winter of 1895–96, he had treated a woman named Emma Eckstein.

The patient suffered from many different anxiety symptoms, including stomach pains and difficulty in walking. Freud, ever the conscientious physician, asked Fliess to come to Vienna to look at Eckstein and confirm that her symptoms were not due to physical problems, that is, a nasal injury she had suffered. After his examination, Fliess decided that nasal surgery was called for, and he performed the operation in late February 1895.

Emma Eckstein no longer complained of stomach pains. Instead, she started experiencing severe pain and bleeding from her nose, and a fetid odor came from the site of the surgery. Two weeks after the operation, Freud, worried and confused, brought a local surgeon to see her. After cleaning around the wound, the surgeon, as Freud later wrote to Fliess, "suddenly pulled at something like thread. He kept right on pulling, and before either of us had time to think, at least half a meter of gauze had been removed from the cavity. The next moment came a flow of blood. The patient turned white, her eyes bulged, and her pulse was no longer palpable." The surgeon quickly repacked the wound, stopping the hemorrhaging. Shaken, Freud fled to the next room, and drank a glass of cognac. When he returned, Eckstein greeted him with the comment, "So this is the strong sex." Freud was horrified at Fliess's incompetent operation. Apparently, the gauze had been left in by mistake and had kept Emma's surgical wound from healing properly.

As a doctor, Freud had seen plenty of blood. What upset him was that "this mishap had happened to you," as Freud carefully put it in a letter to Fliess. In 1895, Freud had very few friends, and he could not bear to separate from Fliess. Instead, he found a way to blame the only other person involved: the patient. A year later, after Eckstein had recovered, Freud reported to Fliess that she was a hysterical bleeder. Eckstein had come back to Freud for further treatment and admitted to a long history of nosebleeds.

Eckstein's bleeding after the operation, Freud explained, was a hysterical bid for attention. Freud went to great pains to exonerate Fliess and to forget the guilty strip of gauze.

Strangely enough, Eckstein forgave Freud for his role in the botched operation and came to believe that her symptoms were psychological, though she was generally unable to walk for the rest of her life. She even became an analyst herself. Freud occasionally corresponded with her for years after her treatment. Much as Freud tried to put Emma Eckstein out of his head, the topic returned to mind, though not his conscious mind. On July 23–24, 1895, five months after Eckstein's operation, Freud had what he called "The Dream of Irma's Injection." Freud analyzed this dream immediately and presented a brief version of it in the *Project for a Scientific Psychology.*

Freud dreamed that he had met his patient, "Irma," in a large hall full of guests. Taking Irma to the side, Freud chided her for not accepting his "solution," saying, "If you still get pains, it's really only your fault." Irma replied that her pains were "choking her." Freud noted that Irma looked pale and puffy, and he looked down her throat. There, in her throat, Freud found whitish scabs on what looked like the bone structure of the nose. Freud called in various doctors to examine Irma, including "Otto" (Oscar Rie, a colleague who had criticized his therapy with Irma the day before) and Fliess. Freud recalled that Otto had carelessly given Irma an injection, probably with a dirty syringe. (In his working life, Freud was quite proud that in the two years he had been injecting an elderly patient with morphine twice daily, that patient had never suffered an infection.)

When Freud analyzed this dream in 1895, he viewed it in terms of a mental primary process, a free-flowing discharge of excess mental energy. This dream, he declared, was simple wish fulfillment: Irma's continued suffering was not his fault, and he was able to take revenge on Otto, whom he could not challenge in real life. Freud did not mention the Eckstein disaster here, or at any other time in his life. In the *Project*, Freud was not ready to discuss the strange distortions and metaphors that form the language of dreams. Still, he had glimpsed that dreams had meaning and that meaning could be revealed when the dreamer awoke. Freud jokingly told Fliess that one day his house would bear a plaque stating, "On July 24, 1895, the secret of the dream was revealed to Dr. Sigmund Freud."

On October 23, 1896, Freud's father died. The death was not unexpected; Jacob Freud was 81 and had been treated for heart failure that summer. Despite Freud's old hostility toward his weak father, the father who simply

The death of his father, Jacob, on October 23, 1896, affected Freud profoundly and spurred him to delve deeper into his own psyche as he began psychoanalysis of himself.

brushed off his cap when a Gentile knocked it into the street, Freud was devastated. In 1896, he was a 40-year-old doctor with a wife and six children and a thriving practice. Yet he wrote to Fliess, "My father's death has affected me profoundly. . . . Now I feel quite uprooted."

His father's death spurred Freud to begin two new projects. One was the writing of *The Interpretation of Dreams,* which was published in 1899. The other work was a far more serious undertaking, which Freud carried on for the rest of his life: his psychoanalysis of himself.

Dr. Sigm. Freud
Docent für Nervenkrankheiten
a. d. Universität

Wien, 21 Sept 97
IX., Berggasse 19.

Theurer Wilhelm

Hier bin ich wieder, seit gestern
früh, frisch, heiter, dürftig unarm, derzeit
beschäftigungslos u. schreibe Dir, nachdem
ich die Herstellung der Wohnbarkeit
und nun will ich Dir sofort das große
Geheimnis anvertrauen, das mir in
den letzten Monaten langsam gedämmert
hat. Ich glaube an meine Neurotica
nicht mehr, das ist wohl nicht ohne Erklärung
verständlich, aber fest, so selbst glaubenswürdig
scheinbar nachdem es zu erzählen könnte.
Ich will also historisch beginnen, woher die
Motive zum Unglauben gekommen
sind, die fortgesetzten Enttäuschungen bei
den Versuchen meine Analyse zum
wirklichen Abschluss zu bringen, das
Auseinanderlaufen der kurze Zeit lang am
besten engagirten Leute, das Ausbleiben
der vollen Erfolge, auf die ich gerechnet
hatte, die Möglichkeit und die theilweisen

Solutions

Freud joined the Vienna B'nai B'rith, a Jewish fraternal organization, in September 1897. The organization's mission was to work on "elevating the mental and moral character of the people of our faith." Here, Freud could enjoy friendship with other Jews without having to attend religious services. Freud quickly added B'nai B'rith's biweekly meetings to his strict schedule. Almost 40 years later, Freud wrote in a letter to members of B'nai B'rith, "I soon became one of you, enjoyed your sympathy, and almost never neglected to go to the place, surrounded by hostility, where I was sure to find friends." Freud gave 21 popular lectures at B'nai B'rith over the years and even remembered one group being "enthusiastic" about his work and showering him with "unrestrained applause"—a vivid contrast to his memories of his other Viennese audiences.

He was glad to have friends; his work and personal life were in turmoil. By 1897, Freud had begun to doubt his seduction theory of hysteria. He had several reasons to question the theory. The first was the fact that his therapy

The first page of the letter Freud sent to Fliess on September 21, 1897, in which Freud begins to express doubts about the validity of some of Fliess's work.

did not seem to fully cure his patients. Many of his patients left midway through their treatment or only partially recovered. Those who remained resisted Freud's attempts to extract what he called their "repressed infantile experiences." The seduction theory also implied that in general the father of the household had brought on the patient's later hysteria. Yet Freud's own brothers and sisters showed hysterical symptoms. Freud could not believe that his father abused his sisters. His mind reeled at the volume of childhood sexual abuse that would have been required to supply him with so many neurotic patients. In September 1897, Freud wrote to Fliess about the "great secret" that he had guessed that summer. Freud had realized that most of his patients' tales of seduction were simply not true.

After abandoning the seduction theory, Freud was able to hear his patients' free associations and lengthy stories not as absolute truths but as a code for some other, deeper message. But what was that message? What was the true basis of mental illness? Freud decided to seek the secrets of mental life in himself.

He had good cause. Since his father's death, Freud had been depressed on and off. He had also suffered various neurotic symptoms during most of his adult life. His heart raced, his stomach ached, and he had migraine headaches. When Freud's work went badly, he would become morose and complain of depression and fatigue. More practically, Freud simply could not complete an analysis on any of his patients. He was his own last, best hope.

Freud was not optimistic. As he wrote to Fliess in November 1897, "I can analyze myself only with objectively gained knowledge. . . . True self-analysis is impossible, else there would be no illness." Freud persevered. Finding clues everywhere, he used many sources for his "objectively gained" knowledge, such as mistakes he made when writing, or mispronunciations he committed while speaking, and episodes when he forgot people's names or quotations from books. These errors are the famed "Freudian slips," mistakes that arise when an unconscious wish or intention overwhelms a conscious one. Freud also analyzed his dreams, and he hunted through his childhood memories.

When Freud looked for clues to the workings of his own mind in his everyday mistakes, he made one of the basic assumptions of psychoanalysis: every action has a cause. Freud did not believe in "random" actions or accept that anyone ever said anything for "no reason at all." Even free association was not really free. Everything the patient said was the result of unconscious processes mixing with everyday events. In Freudian psychology, there is very little free will.

Once Freud started looking into his own memories, they returned en masse. Freud suddenly remembered his Catholic nurse, his rivalry with his nephews and siblings, and a glimpse of his mother's genitals during a train journey when he was four. Freud's memories of the nurse who toilet trained him were especially important. He was able to confirm many of his remembered experiences with the nurse by questioning his mother. Though the seduction theory was inaccurate, Freud thought, his mother's confirmations of these early events showed that psychoanalytical techniques could be used to uncover actual childhood memories—especially sexual memories.

Freud found evidence of infants' sexual urges in his own life. He had loved and desired his mother as a child, and wished that his father and siblings and other rivals would die so that he could have his mother to himself. Freud later titled this set of conflicts the Oedipus complex. According to Greek myth, Oedipus, abandoned at birth and raised by strangers, later unwittingly killed his father and then married his mother. Both infantile sexuality and the "family drama" of the Oedipus complex came to play a central role in Freud's later theories of child development.

In a paper published in 1898, Freud wrote, "We do wrong to ignore the sexual life of children entirely; in my experience, children are capable of every psychical activity, and many somatic [bodily] ones as well." This focus on desire instead of on trauma was a significant shift in Freud's thinking. He always believed that some neuroses were caused by genuine trauma. In the 1890s, he was certain that at least two of his female patients had been assaulted by their fathers. But most neuroses, in his view, were caused by the movement of sexual energy *within* the child.

While he was searching his memory, Freud was also dreaming. He often remembered his dreams and had kept a journal of them years before. With "The Dream of Irma's Injection," Freud began to see dreams as the fulfillments of wishes. However, he also realized that many dreams are nightmares, and frankly unpleasant. After much thought, Freud concluded that dreams are not always expressions of conscious wishes. There must be a second level of motivation, very different types of wishes from those that people allow themselves to recognize.

All dreams contain some common elements, Freud wrote. Each dream begins with a childhood memory, perhaps of the Oedipus complex or some other emotionally charged experience. Over the course of the previous day, the dreamer will have had a few experiences that seem to be related to those memories. These events form the "day residue" in the dream. Together, the childhood memories and the day residue make up the underlying content of the dream.

If dreams were only stuck-together bits of memories and yesterday's lunch, dream interpretation would be fairly simple. But often childhood wishes and memories have been repressed and hidden from consciousness. The dreamer has constructed a defense against knowing his or her true wishes. In dreams, these desires are hidden by an inner censor, which distorts the dream's meaning in several ways. The censor may condense the features of many different people into one character. Alternately, the censor may transfer one person's comments or actions onto another in the dream. The censor may substitute symbols for characters in the dreams; a father may become a king, a mother a cupboard, a child an animal. The censor turns verbal thoughts into visual images. Other symbols can take the form of verbal cues and puns. As an example, Freud cited the case of a man who dreamed of a broken bone when he was concerned about a broken marriage.

By the time the dream emerges from these processes, the *latent* content, or inner conflict of the unconscious, has been disguised and transformed into the symbolic or *manifest* content. When the dreamer awakes, the dream undergoes another revision. The dreamer forces a logical structure onto the dream so that it is intelligible. In the end, Freud wrote, "A dream is the (disguised) fulfillment of a (suppressed, repressed) wish."

Since the dreamer's true wishes never appear in the dream, a dream interpreter must puzzle out the unpredictable transformations of the latent content. In *The Interpretation of Dreams*, Freud described several ways that wishes can lead to nightmares. The most common category was the set of dreams experienced by patients who wanted to disprove Freud's theories. A more common type of unpleasant dream was the anxiety dream. Freud claimed that some anxiety dreams are the result of sexual wishes, where sexual energy, or libido, is changed into anxiety, especially when the wish is revealed too clearly in the dream. In other anxiety dreams, the worry or fear is present before the dream begins. Then the anxiety is used like any other day residue, to expose a repressed wish.

Freud did not believe that all dreams were the result of sexual wishes. Dreams of hunger and other needs showed up in *The Interpretation of Dreams*. Only later did Freud conclude that all dreams without an *obvious* meaning were sexual in nature.

Freud enjoyed his work on dreams. Interpreting a dream involved solving riddles, puns, and jokes—except in the case of children's dreams. Children have not yet formed internal censors, and their dreams are pure, unadulterated wish fulfillment. Freud's youngest daughter, Anna, once was starved for a day, after she gorged on strawberries and vomited. That night, the 19-month-old called out in her sleep, in childish German phrases roughly translated as "Anna Freud, stwawberries, wild stwawberries, omlet, pudden!" Anna announced her ideal menu in her dreams and doubly emphasized her favorite food.

The Interpretation of Dreams was published in 1899. It is without doubt Freud's most important and popular work. As Freud wrote in a later edition, "The interpretation of dreams is the royal road to knowledge of the unconscious activities of the mind." The book received some excellent reviews, though some critics agreed with Freud's own comment to Fliess that "there is too much that is new and unbelievable and too little strict proof."

Like his case studies, Freud's dream analyses were masterpieces of close observation and careful thought. Each dream and dreamer were unique, but each also provided clear illustrations of some larger principle. Yet like Freud's case studies, the dream analyses had no predictive power. Freud could not examine a person's life and tell what sorts of dreams he or she would have. All of his interpretations were done after the dream had taken place. The only "proof" we have that Freud's interpretations are correct is how believable they seem.

Taken together, Freud's dream work, his work on Freudian slips, the Oedipus complex, and his theories of infantile sexuality form a new vision of the mind. In this view, unconscious desires dominate human dreams, neurotic symptoms, and every simple mistake. These wishes constantly enter our everyday lives; we can read them if we only choose to do so. The source of these desires is the unrelenting biological urge to reproduce. The age-old distinction between mind and body, or nature and soul, now became useless to Freud. The unconscious lurked at the bottom of every thought.

By the time Freud finished *The Interpretation of Dreams*, he had been analyzing himself for nearly three years. This intense self-examination did not keep Freud from being nervous, moody, and depressed when the book first came out. Freud complained that his book was ignored and misunderstood. He worried about his finances and bemoaned the fact that he was 44 and generally unnoticed. Freud was unhappy, but he was also undergoing a profound transition. He was losing his second father.

Freud was becoming less and less enchanted with Fliess. He started writing fewer and shorter letters to the man he once called "Dearest Wilhelm." At the beginning, Freud had cherished his friend's support and advice. Over time, though, their relationship became less cordial and more competitive. Freud wrote in a preface to the second edition of *The Interpretation of Dreams* in 1908 about "my reaction to my father's death, that is, the most significant event, the most decisive loss of a man's life." After Jacob Freud died, the main father figure in Freud's life was Fliess. As with Brücke and Breuer before, Freud would soon need to rebel, to put this "father" in his place.

In September 1901, Freud managed to escape his own moods by traveling to Rome. He had dreamed of visiting Rome for his entire life but never had the courage to actually go there. From his schoolboy obsession with Hannibal to his collection of Roman art and antiques, Freud was consistently drawn to this ancient center of civilization. He spent months studying maps of Rome over the years, and he traveled extensively in northern and central Italy. He later called his first visit to Rome the "high point of my life." He admired works by Leonardo da Vinci and Michelangelo and visited the Vatican and the Roman catacombs, a vast network of underground passages used by early Christians for worship and burial. He visited Rome several more times in his life, but this first trip made the greatest impression. He was gaining the courage to travel wherever he wished—and defend his academic career.

While he was writing *Studies on Hysteria* and *The Interpretation of Dreams*, Freud was either neglecting or ignoring his shaky position at the University of Vienna. Back in 1885, before he had traveled to work with Charcot, Freud had been granted the position of *privatdozent*, a sort of junior professor. Freud gave lectures on neurology, his specialty, at the university, without pay. He simply did not have enough powerful friends to push his career further. While the average privatdozent waited about 8 years to be declared *ausserordentlicher professor* (extraordinary professor), by 1901 Freud had waited 11 years. In 1897, the medical faculty had approved of his promotion by a vote of 22 to 10. However, to be declared ausserordentlicher professor, a candidate needed the approval of the Ministry of Education, which failed to act in Freud's case.

Freud was reluctant to help himself. He dreamed of being a scientist famed for his brilliant theories, not for his self-promotion. But Freud was a Jew at a time when the mayor of Vienna, Karl Lueger, and other prominent Austrian politicians were fanning anti-Jewish hatred. Freud's theories of sexuality and hysteria, his old fascination with cocaine, even his championing of Charcot, had earned him enemies. When one of Freud's old professors advised him to find a "personal counterinfluence," Freud finally began to look for help.

Having spent much of the previous decade treating the wives, daughters, and widows of Vienna's wealthy ruling classes, Freud was well armed. Ultimately, one of his former patients, the Baroness Ferstel, convinced the Ministry of Education to grant the professorship to her cherished physician, in exchange for a painting from her private gallery.

With the promotion to ausserordentlicher professor, Freud climbed in status. The promotion was a vote of confidence for Freud from the medical faculty, and he was able to charge higher fees. After the whole ordeal was over, Freud lamented, "If I had taken those few steps three years ago, I should have been appointed three years earlier, and should have spared myself much. Others are just as clever, without having to go to Rome first."

Freud had needed time to overcome the pride that had kept him from asking friends for help. In later years, Freud's courage and political pragmatism would ensure the survival of his ideas and of the psychoanalytic movement.

CHAPTER

7

Interactions

By the time Freud published *Three Essays on the Theory of Sexuality* in 1905, he was no longer hesitant about his theories, his own importance, or politicking on his own behalf. He had published *The Interpretation of Dreams* and received his professorship. These triumphs nourished him through his next tragedy, his break with Wilhelm Fliess.

Freud and Fliess's relationship had been strained since 1897, when Freud had begun to construct a psychological theory of dreams while Fliess remained a staunch biologist. The simmering conflict boiled over when Freud and Fliess met in the summer of 1900. Fliess suggested that periodic processes—biological events that run in cycles, like menstruation—influenced the mind. In particular, he said that this vital periodicity must affect the course of mental illness, including the illnesses Freud was treating through his psychoanalytic therapy.

Freud, astonished and hurt, protested that Fliess was undermining the entire value of his work. What was the use of therapy if an illness were controlled by some internal clock? In response, a bewildered Fliess accused Freud of putting his own thoughts into his patients' minds. During

Freud with his wife and mother during a summer vacation at a mountain resort in 1905. Freud's mother was a strong and energetic presence in the Freud household throughout her life.

that awful summer visit, Freud also commented that neuroses could only be solved by a theory grounded in each person's basic bisexuality. Fliess objected that he had said the same thing two and a half years earlier, when Freud refused to believe it.

Shortly after this meeting, Freud and Fliess's relationship began to unravel. Freud seemed to be using Fliess, alternately rejecting and co-opting his ideas at his convenience. Freud did attempt to win his friend back at first, offering to coauthor a book titled *Bisexuality in Man*, but Fliess did not bite. The two had stopped exchanging letters by 1902. In 1903, a young associate of Freud's named Otto Weininger published a book entitled *Sex and Character*, which stole outright many of Fliess's ideas on bisexuality. Fliess immediately recognized Freud's hand in the crime. Freud denied the charges at first, then claimed that many authors had written about bisexuality before Fliess. The appearance of another—probably plagiarized—book by Weininger's friend Hermann Swoboda, which discussed vital periods of 23 and 28 days, ended Freud and Fliess's relationship altogether.

It is ironic that Freud's relationship with Fliess ended in this way. After all, Freud had been a victim of the same sort of academic thievery when he was young, concerning the anesthetic properties of cocaine. Freud thus attacked Fliess with the sharpest weapon that Freud himself had ever endured. Freud was truly no longer afraid of his power, even his power to wound his friends.

In 1902, a young physician named Wilhelm Stekel suggested that Freud meet weekly with other professionals who were interested in psychoanalysis. The group, called the Wednesday Psychological Society, finally gave Freud an audience that was eager and willing to hear his ideas. Each week, the group would hear a paper by one of its members, eat pastry, smoke, and discuss the topic before them. Freud, the founding father of psychoanalysis, would always have the last word.

Members brought newcomers to the group, and the society flourished. By 1906, there were 17 members and about a dozen attendees at each meeting. In October, the society hired Otto Rank, a self-taught psychologist who was close to Freud, to take notes on the meetings. By 1907, though, the society was a shambles. The members competed for Freud's attention, jealously guarded the ownership of their ideas, and insulted each other's work. Many writers have compared them to a large family of sons, all competing for their father's love. Freud was disappointed in his followers. One German visitor noted charitably that Freud had a reputation for such wild theories that very few respectable doctors would attend his meetings at all. In 1908, Freud's group reorganized as the Vienna Psychoanalytic Society.

With a crowd of supporters surrounding him, Freud began to form his most controversial theories on infantile sexuality. He was not the first author to write on sexuality or even the first writer to describe childhood sexual urges. Several doctors had published discussions of the relationships between thumb sucking, toilet training, and children's character development. But Freud was prepared to present a complete theory of sexual development.

In the first edition of *The Interpretation of Dreams*, Freud had commented, "We think highly of the happiness of childhood because it is still innocent of sexual desires." Five years later, however, in *Three Essays on the Theory of Sexuality,* Freud amended that statement, claiming that it was true only of children in the latency stage. Freud described three stages of sexual development: a sexually active stage from birth to age five; a latency stage from five until puberty, during which children forget and ignore their sexuality; and the adult sexual stage, starting at puberty.

The infantile sexual stage was not supposed to be identical to adult sexuality. According to Freud, children find sexual pleasure in many activities, such as thumb sucking, patting and touching themselves, retaining and passing feces, and masturbating. Since children could gain sexual pleasure in so many different ways, Freud claimed they were polymorphously perverse, meaning that there is the potential for all possible perversions in each child. Freud used the word *perversion* to define the practice of seeking pleasure in objects or animals instead of human partners, and the desire for anything other than heterosexual sexual intercourse. He believed that these perversions could also develop in adults under special circumstances; these practices included exhibitionism (exposing the genitals to an audience), fetishism (gaining pleasure from objects, such as shoes), and masochism (getting pleasure from pain or abuse).

Freud thought that children went through several phases where their sexuality focused on particular parts of the body. The first stage is the autoerotic (self-pleasure) stage. Children generally get their gratification from sucking at first, though any part of their bodies could produce sexual pleasure. This is the oral stage. During the next stage, which frequently occurs at about the same time as toilet training, children derive sexual pleasure from the anus and retaining feces. Finally, after the anal stage, children's main source of pleasure switches to the genitals, where it remains for the rest of their lives. During latency, children have an "amnesia" about their previous sexual development. Instead of exploring their bodies, these school-age children sublimate, or redirect, their sexual energy into other activities, such as school and play.

Over the next decade, Freud came to define the differences between hysteria and obsession in terms of these infantile sexual stages. He believed that obsessives regress to the anal stage, when the child first begins to express anger and a need for control. Hysterics, on the other hand, regress to previous love-objects, usually a parent, and reject adult sexuality altogether. In the *Three Essays*, Freud describes adolescent sexual development. During puberty, the focus of sexual energy, or libido, shifts from the self to others. The adolescent now wants to involve other people in his or her sexual acts. At first, though, adolescents only fantasize about the objects of their sexual urges. This fantasy life revives old libidinal ties to the parents. To progress beyond fantasy, the adult must break free from parental authority. Adult sexual urges come to focus on the genitals, while sexual activities involving other parts of the body take their place as "pre-pleasures." These "pre-pleasures" motivate the adult to pursue the "end-pleasure" of orgasm. Freud stated that this end-pleasure appeared only at puberty.

Freud's *Three Essays* were problematic for many reasons. He never really defined "pleasure" or "excitation." The essays are also full of the prevailing prejudices about women's sexuality. While men simply gain pleasure from their penises, women must repress their sexuality by transferring their pleasure from the infantile "masculine" sexual zone of the external sex organ, the clitoris, to the internal organ, the vagina. This demand that women sacrifice a major source of adult sexual pleasure has hurt both women and their psychotherapists since Freud first thought of it. Women, Freud also suggested, must go through more stages than men to reach maturity, an idea some biographers attribute to the Victorian stereotype of the weak, irrational woman who needs to be controlled.

Though Freud declared in *Three Essays* that heterosexual intercourse with a loved partner was the ultimate sexual goal, he did not think that either marriage or single-partner relationships were necessary for mental health. He favored free sexual coupling for young men and women and despaired at the lack of effective contraceptives. Still, in the Freud household, psychoanalysis stopped at the nursery door, as Freud said. Freud's theories had very little effect on his home life. He scolded his son for masturbating and most likely remained faithful to his wife, though he noticed that his family developed the same sorts of minor hysterias and neuroses as everyone else. The one family member who was profoundly affected by his theories was his youngest daughter, Anna, who later became a psychoanalyst.

In the meantime, Freud was learning from his clinical patients. Three of Freud's most famous patients from this period were Dora, a hysteric, Rat Man, an obsessive, and Little Hans, a five-year-old boy who developed a crippling fear, called a *phobia*. These case studies illustrate how Freud was thinking about his patients and how he went about curing them. By the turn of the century, Freud was no longer pressing his patients' foreheads and commanding them to "Remember!" Freud sat in a chair behind the couch where his patients relaxed and free-associated. This arrangement was extremely useful; Freud's patients were free to talk

The couch in Freud's office, where patients rested and told the doctor their innermost thoughts. Freud sat out of sight.

without seeing his reactions. Freud also admitted, "I cannot stand being stared at eight hours a day (or longer) by others." Freud believed that analysts should never take notes during psychoanalytic sessions. The analyst needed to focus his entire attention on his patients to collect any and all information on the patients' minds, from their symptoms to their dreams to the misspelled words in their letters.

In 1905, Freud published a case history that he had recorded five years before, called "Fragments of an Analysis of a Case of Hysteria." Freud had analyzed a young woman he called Dora, the 18-year-old Ida Bauer, who suffered from common hysterical symptoms such as migraine headaches, laryngitis, and a nervous cough. At the time, Freud was very interested in demonstrating his theories of hysteria and dream symbols with a real, live patient. Dora seemed like an excellent candidate.

Dora readily explained how she came to be in her sorry state. Dora's mother spent her days obsessively cleaning the house, avoiding both her husband and daughter. When Dora was 16, an old friend of the family, Mr. K., had made sexual advances toward her. Dora, shocked and repulsed, had slapped him. When Dora told her father, though, he took Mr. K.'s word over Dora's, dismissing her as an adolescent with too much sex on her mind. Freud did not take sides when Dora first told him her story, and he soon found out that Dora's father was carrying on an affair with Mrs. K. Dora and Mrs. K. had been very close friends, and Mrs. K. had been Dora's confidante. They had slept in the same bed when the families vacationed together. Dora spoke of Mrs. K's "adorable white body" during her analysis. Furthermore, Mr. K. had assaulted Dora more than once. When Dora was 14, Mr. K. had caught her in his office and kissed her passionately on the lips. Naturally, the young girl was revolted by the old man's lechery—or was she?

Freud could not accept Dora's disgust. Always rebelling against middle-class social morality, Freud insisted that Dora felt sexual excitement when Mr. K. attacked her. This sort of hidden desire is not impossible. However, it is also not what Dora was describing to Freud. Attacked by a friend, betrayed by her father, Dora was adrift in a hostile world. Soon, that world included Freud. Dora grew tired of Freud's resistance to her testimony and left abruptly after 11 months of analysis. She rejected Freud, the same way she had rejected Mr. K.

Dora's case is important not only because Freud, normally a careful, attentive listener, failed to understand Dora's feelings about her life but because her case demonstrated to Freud the perils of transference and countertransference. In psychoanalytic terms, *transference* occurs when patients bring their feelings from some other situation in life to their relationship with their analysts. Dora returned to Freud's office once in 1902, and essentially admitted that she had projected her fury at Mr. K. onto Freud. By contrast, *countertransference* takes place when analysts project their preexisting emotions onto their patients. Both transference and countertransference are inescapable results of any analysis, but if they are acknowledged, they can help both parties explore the patient's unconscious wishes. Freud did not admit that he experienced a countertransference with Dora, and he only began to use the word in 1910. He did come to recognize that unacknowledged countertransference could derail analysis, because it destroys the analyst's neutrality.

It is not clear why Freud experienced such a strong hostile countertransference to Dora. Some authors suggest that Freud himself identified with Mr. K., the masculine aggressor. At the time that he was writing the "Fragment," Freud was losing touch with Fliess, a man who emphasized human bisexuality and was later remembered by Freud as having given him a "homosexual charge." In Dora's case, Freud wrote in a postscript to the "Fragment," "I failed to discover in time and to inform the patient that her homosexual . . . love for Mrs. K. was the strongest unconscious current in her mental life." At the time, Freud was not interested in the "feminine" side of life; he was rejecting his attraction to Fliess and ignoring Dora's desire for Mrs. K. (whom Mr. K. had rejected).

In 1904, Freud became acquainted with a 30-year-old Swiss psychiatrist who sent him a paper on the applications of Freudian ideas to schizophrenia, a mental illness in which patients lose their grasp on reality and commonly "hear voices." Freud admired the paper and immediately began corresponding with this new colleague, Dr. Carl Gustav Jung. Jung worked at the psychiatric clinic at the University of Zurich, Switzerland, with Eugene Bleuler, the psychiatric researcher who had coined the term schizophrenia.

From their very first letters, there were signs that Freud and Jung's relationship would be troubled. In the preface to the paper he sent to Freud, Jung mentioned that he did not believe that childhood sexual trauma was the sole cause of mental illness, a direct contradiction of Freud's position. Still, Freud was impressed with Jung. Jung had a long career ahead of him, he was brighter than most of Freud's Viennese followers, and perhaps most importantly, he was neither Austrian nor Jewish. Between 1906 and 1910, Freud began to enjoy an international reputation, and foreigners such as the Englishman Ernest Jones and the Hungarian Sándor Ferenczi began to join his circle. Yet Freud felt that Jung, and only Jung, could carry on the movement. Freud desperately wanted psychoanalytic ideas to spread beyond his small, mostly Jewish Viennese clique. Otherwise, he felt, all his work would be ignored and forgotten, crushed by anti-Semitism. Who could better spread Freud's ideas than the tall, blue-eyed Jung, whose father was a Christian pastor? Jung became Freud's crown prince. He also became a partial replacement for Fliess, judging by the intensity of Freud and Jung's emotional correspondence.

In 1904, Freud began a lengthy correspondence with Swiss doctor Carl Jung, who had begun using Freud's ideas in his treatment of schizophrenics.

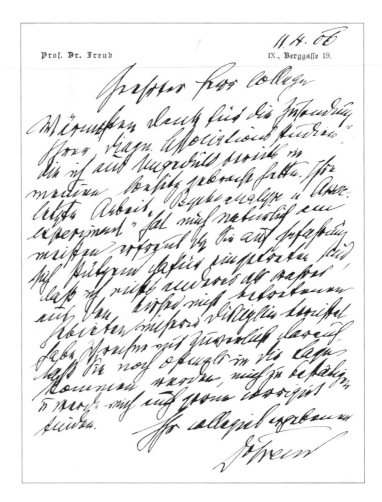

Freud and Jung did not meet in person until 1907, the year of Freud's analysis of his most famous case of obsession, the so-called Rat Man. When this patient, a 29-year-old lawyer, came to Freud, his mind was filled with fear that some tragedy would befall his father or the woman he was courting, or that he would kill someone or cut his own throat. He had finally come to Freud because of his terror over a story he had recently heard during his army training. According to his captain, in some unidentified country in the Orient judges ordered a particularly awful form of torture for criminals. A criminal would be tied down, and a pot with a large rat in it would be placed over the victim's buttocks. Prodded by a red-hot poker, the rat would begin to chew. "Into the anus," Freud interrupted. At that point, the patient's face showed a confused look of pleasure and disgust.

The key to Freud's analysis was the German word for "rat," *Ratte*. As in dreams, the unconscious frequently makes puns on important words. In this case, the patient linked the word *Ratte* with *heiraten* (to marry) and *Spielratte* (gambling rat), a reference to his father's gambling debts in his youth.

When the Rat Man had first had sexual intercourse, he had thought, "This is great! I could murder my father for this!" Over the course of the analysis, the Rat Man admitted that when he was between three and four, his father had beaten him for masturbating. He had sworn at his father vehemently, with all the words his small mind could muster, calling out "You towel! You plate!" because he did not know any curses at the time. The Rat Man saw his father as interfering with his sex life, and the story of the rat torture brought to mind his conflicting love and hate for his father. Once the Rat Man understood this interpretation, his obsessive symptoms disappeared.

Freud's other famous case from this period was a very different sort of patient. Little Hans was a phobic, paralyzed by fear, and he was only five years old. At first, he was not directly interviewed by Freud. All of Freud's information was provided by Max Graf, the child's father and a member of the Wednesday Psychological Society. The Grafs tried to raise their child without the usual sexual prejudices, but like the Freuds, they fell back on typical child-rearing practices of the time. When Mrs. Graf had a second child, the Grafs explained that the stork had visited them, a story that Hans, a bright boy, did not believe for a minute.

Graf brought Hans to Freud after Hans developed a fear that horses would bite him. This was a difficult problem for a child in Vienna before the mass production of automobiles. The terrifying beasts were on every street. Hans's fear began to spread from horses to all large animals, though small animals were still safe. Hans was also becoming more and more interested in genitalia, and Hans's father thought that the boy might be afraid of big animals' large penises. Max Graf discussed the topic with Hans, telling him that big animals have big penises, just as little animals have small penises. Hans's reply was a masterpiece of childhood reasoning: "And all people have wi-wi-makers [Hans's word for penis]. And my wi-wi-maker is growing with me when I get bigger. After all, it's attached." Hans's statement that all people have penises (with no regard for a person's sex) is amusing, but Freud saw a deeper meaning. Hans's clear declaration that his penis was attached showed that he was concerned that his penis might become detached or lost. Freud thought that Hans suffered from castration anxiety.

Who would castrate poor little Hans? The answer lay, again, in a symbol provided by Hans's unconscious mind. Hans's father had a large black mustache, which looked to Hans like the muzzle of a big black horse. Hans, at age five, was in the midst of the Oedipus complex. He loved his mother and wished that his father would die so he would not have to share her. If his father found out about Hans's wishes, though, Hans thought his father would cut off his penis. Eventually, Hans conquered his fears by coming up with a scheme to keep both his mother and father. Hans could marry his mother, and Hans's father could marry *his* mother.

Hans recovered from his phobia and grew up to be a successful director of operas. When he visited Freud in 1922, he read his own case study and commented that he did not remember the therapy at all. It was, he said, like reading about a stranger. Clearly, Hans's conflict had receded back into the unconscious, where it belonged.

Freud's analyses of these three cases were influenced by his view of masculinity and femininity. Dora, like all women, was supposed to submit to male authority, passively accepting Mr. K.'s advances. Men, on the other hand, must reject their feminine or homosexual tendencies and break free of their father's authority, despite the fact that they desire their father's love. Freud continued to struggle with these issues in his theories and his own relationships with his disciples through the end of World War I.

Clark University Worcester (Mass.)   Celebration of the Psychological L

'09

Holt   Whipple Kirkpatrick   Wilson
                                                              Sanford   God

In September 1909, Freud (front row, fifth from left) made his first and only visit to the United States at the invitation of Clark University in Worcester, Massachusetts. He delivered a series of lectures there and is seen here with the members of Clark's psychology department.

Reality

By 1909, Freud's work was in demand. The previous year, he had published articles on bisexuality, hysteria, children's sexual development, and the effect of middle-class sexual morality on mental illness. The Vienna Psychoanalytic Society was flourishing. Freud now had the money to begin collecting antiques, rugs, and sculpture from ancient civilizations. Hanns Sachs, Freud's friend and colleague, said that Freud's office began to remind him not of "a doctor's office but rather of an archeologist's study."

Freud's fame was spreading, even reaching the United States. In 1909, G. Stanley Hall, the president of Clark University in Worcester, Massachusetts, invited Freud to give a series of lectures there. He had heard of Freud from a visiting researcher who worked at the same Swiss hospital as Jung. Hall was delighted with Freud's scandalous ideas on sex and cited Freud's ideas in his book on adolescence, much to the disgust of his reviewers. Hall also invited Jung, who was a well-known expert on schizophrenia. In the end, Sándor Ferenczi, a regular attendee at the Vienna Psychoanalytic Society and a good friend, went as well.

At first, Freud was none too happy to go. He felt that Americans were prudish about sex and stingy with their money. However, when Hall raised Freud's travel stipend, Freud decided to make the journey. On the way to the United States, Freud, Jung, and Ferenczi had lunch together at the German port of Bremen before boarding the ship. Jung could not stop talking about an archeological dig. Freud, alarmed, thought that Jung's obsessive monologue on old, dead bones was proof of Jung's death wish against him, and Freud fainted. But the remainder of the trip went smoothly. Freud complained that American food upset his stomach, but he was able to meet with William James and James Putnam, Harvard professors of psychology and neurology, respectively. James, the author of *The Varieties of Religious Experience*, was disturbed by Freud's outright rejection of religion. Putnam, on the other hand, worked at Massachusetts General Hospital, treating hysterics. Meeting and talking to Freud convinced him that psychoanalysis was the best treatment for hysterical patients. Freud's conquest of American psychiatry had begun.

Freud was warmly welcomed in the United States. When he returned to Vienna, though, he was confronted by open warfare. Freud and his many followers met in Nuremberg, Germany, in the spring of 1910. Freud wanted to ensure that psychoanalytic ideas would continue to spread throughout the world, under Jung's guidance, but he also wanted to avoid snubbing his Viennese adherents. At the Nuremberg congress, Freud had Ferenczi propose the creation of an International Psychoanalytic Association in addition to the Viennese Psychoanalytic Association. Jung was to be the new organization's permanent president.

The Viennese were outraged, much as a child might be when a wonderful present is given to an envied younger brother. Eventually, after Freud personally begged the Viennese group to save psychoanalysis by recruiting more Gentiles (non-Jews), Freud and his followers agreed on a compromise. Jung would be president of the international association for two years, and Alfred Adler, a Viennese and an original Wednesday Psychological Society member, would become president of the Vienna Psychoanalytic Society, replacing Freud.

The truce did not last long. In a later publication, *Civilization and its Discontents*, Freud quoted the German author Heinrich Heine, who wrote, "One must . . . forgive one's enemies—but not before they have been hanged." Alfred Adler had his own theories of neurosis, which directly contradicted Freud's. Adler believed that people try to make up for having abnormal organs by overcompensating. For example, he observed that many family members of certain great artists have chronic eye ailments. Adler spent much time and energy developing the idea that this "organ inferiority" plays an important role in mental illness. This theory did not upset Freud, but Adler took his thoughts a few steps further, into Fliess's realm. All individuals show features of both sexes, Adler said. Yet neurotics seem to display more secondary sexual characteristics of the opposite sex than others, such as facial hair in women or breast development in men. Neurotics become ill, Adler claimed, when their masculine and feminine tendencies battle. In men, this battle is the "masculine protest" against their passive feminine tendencies. Of course, these tendencies were supposed to be affected by vital periodicity. Adler also suggested that there might be an aggressive drive, which he called the "will to power," in addition to Freud's cherished libido. Both of these concepts, to Adler, emphasized reality and conscious processes, not the unconscious life that Freud believed was all-important.

In Freud's opinion, Adler's theory of the aggressive drive was his worst offense. Freud viewed any talk of human motivation that did not mention childhood sexuality as treachery. He had worked long and hard to

Alfred Adler succeeded Freud as president of the Vienna Psychoanalytic Society. Adler battled with Freud over theoretical differences and eventually resigned from the society in protest.

make people listen to his disturbing theories. A person who started adding new drives to the psyche was, in Freud's opinion, simply trying to pretend that childhood sexual conflicts were not important. Adler's aggressive drive was not just a theoretical mistake, in Freud's mind, but a denial of his most important ideas.

The problem with Adler's ideas, in Freud's view, was that they were not really psychological. Instead of using Freud's terminology, Adler explained neuroses only in bisexual terms. Of course, Freud also explained mental illness in terms of sex, but he described it in terms of libido (sexual energy), which was not biologically defined. In Adler's understanding, all psychology was explained by biology. The mind was a slave, the unconscious was irrelevant, and libido was a bit player.

Adler presented his ideas to the Vienna Psychoanalytic Society in two meetings in 1911, and Freud responded in two more meetings. Those present called the meetings a "trial." One observer wrote that Freud "did not spare his opponent and was not afraid of using sharp words and cutting remarks." Freud accused Adler of having only trivial original ideas and taking the rest of his theories from Freud's own work. Within a year, Freud was calling Adler's ideas "retrogressive." Many of the society's members were upset by Freud's sharp attacks; according to Hanns Sachs, they were afraid that Freud had "violated the freedom of science." Adler resigned his presidency and left the society in 1911, taking nine members with him to form the Society for Free Psychoanalysis. Freud's society voted that members could not belong to both groups, effectively shutting down all communication.

In Vienna, the feud divided fashionable society. Couples had to be reseated at dinner parties to avoid their opponents, and members' wives stopped speaking to each other. Adler went on to develop his own school of psychoanalytic theory, known as individual psychology, and popularized the idea that one's place in the family birth order, as oldest, youngest, or only child, has a profound effect on personality.

By the time Adler left, Freud was ready to see him go. Soon, though, Freud was to part with a colleague he could hardly bear to lose. Carl Jung, too, was questioning Freud's assumptions. Like Adler, Jung was uncomfortable with a strictly sexual definition of libido. Jung preferred to have the term stand for all mental energy, a position Freud once again interpreted as denying the importance of sexuality in development and neurosis. Freud was not willing to see his theory changed by anyone, not even his crown prince. By 1910, Freud and Jung's correspondence was filled with Jung's complaints, insults, and subsequent apologies. Freud, for his part, tried to soothe Jung and offer fatherly advice.

Freud and Jung's relationship became stormier and stormier. In 1912, at Ernest Jones's suggestion, Freud formed a small secret committee to review all new developments in psychoanalysis, particularly work on the unconscious, repression, and infantile sexuality. Jones, Sándor Ferenczi, and Otto Rank were all invited to join the committee. Jung was not.

Meanwhile, Jung was also beginning to doubt Freud's views on infantile sexuality. "Obtaining pleasure is by no means identical with sexuality," he wrote. Jung compared human infancy to the caterpillar stage in butterflies, which is asexual and mostly concerned with eating. Jung attacked all of Freud's most precious ideas, and he did not spare the Oedipus complex. To Jung, the mother was not a sex object, but a protective, nourishing figure. Jung emphasized that current psychological conflicts, not childhood experiences, are the source of most mental illness. A child was much more likely to become neurotic by facing bullies at school than by repressing an infantile wish.

Carl Jung was seen by many as Freud's "crown prince," destined to inherit the leadership of Freud's psychoanalytic movement, until theoretical differences led to a bitter parting.

Jung's idea of the libido had traveled even further from Freud's Vienna consulting room. The not necessarily sexual libido expresses itself, Jung claimed, only through symbols. These symbols are universal and found throughout the world, and they can be discovered by comparing myths from different civilizations.

One of Jung's departures from Freud's orthodoxy, though, has played an enormously influential role in Freudian psychoanalysis up to the present day. By 1912, Jung had come to believe that a patient can be helped only if his or her analyst is emotionally sound. He wrote, "It is quite impossible, even by the subtlest analysis, to prevent the patient from taking over instinctively the way in which his analyst deals with the problems of life. . . . [To avoid the] unacknowledged infantile demands of the analyst . . . [becoming] the parallel demands of the patient . . . [the ana-lyst should undergo] a rigorous analysis at the hands of another." In short, analysts should be analyzed themselves before they analyze others. Subtly, Jung was undermining the value of Freud's self-analysis. Outwardly, he was propos-ing a shift in policy that later helped to standardize the training of analysts. The International Psychoanalytic Association finally adopted his rule 14 years later, in 1926.

Freud and Jung's personal relationship began to deterio-rate. Jung gave a series of lectures in the United States in September 1912, detailing his "heretical" notions. In November, Freud again fainted in front of Jung, this time when the two were discussing psychoanalytic papers Jung had published without citing Freud's work. Jung continued to send angry letters to a bewildered Freud. Having devel-oped his own psychology of dreams and the unconscious, Jung was eager to leave Freud's world.

In 1913, though, Jung was still president of the International Psychoanalytic Association. As the head of the IPA, Jung had prestige and power. Whatever his quarrel with Freud, Jung was not eager to leave his position and did not resign until April 1914. In June Freud published his *History of the Psychoanalytic Movement*. The book was part propaganda, part revenge. Freud explained his version of the development of psychoanalysis in the *History* and spent many pages denouncing Jung, Adler, and other rebels.

Over the next several years, Freud spent endless hours refuting and rejecting others' claims. Much of his work through 1918 and beyond is a response to some foe, generally an opponent chosen from within his own circle of followers. Freud really had very little tolerance for the thoughts of others: If his disciples were not denying his basic findings, then they were stealing his ideas; if they were not either denying basic principles or stealing his work, their papers were dull and unoriginal, and Freud was disappointed in them. Freud, now the "father" of psychoanalysis, seems to have been frightened that his most energetic "sons" would destroy him in a mass Oedipal frenzy.

Given the fighting within the ranks, Freud naturally became concerned with the quality of psychoanalytic therapy. His ideas and terminology were achieving popularity among physicians, who applied them to patients willy-nilly. In 1910, Freud published a pamphlet about these problems entitled "Wild Analysis." The paper begins with the story of a divorced, middle-aged woman who had anxiety

After many challenges to Freud's ideas by Adler, Jung, and others, Freud (front row, left) formed a committee of his supporters to review and monitor all new work done in the field.

symptoms. When she visited her doctor, she was abruptly told that she was "sexually needy," and commanded to either return to her husband, find a boyfriend, or masturbate. The doctor then sent her to Freud to confirm his opinion.

Freud was furious at the doctor's shallow, unthinking diagnosis. To begin with, Freud objected that in psychoanalysis "sex" means more than mere sexual intercourse and includes a world of feeling and anger. Psychoanalytic technique, Freud emphasized, involved not only telling the patient what was wrong but also overcoming resistance, something the careless physician had clearly failed to do. Merely identifying the cause of a problem would not bring a cure if the patient did not accept the judgment.

Freud's most helpful article for the average psychoanalyst is called "On Beginning the Treatment." Instead of just warning and scolding his followers, Freud began to describe how psychoanalytic practice should be conducted. Psychoanalysis should only be undertaken, he said, when a patient is intelligent and his or her behavior is stable, and only after a trial period of a week or so. The analyst should say very little during the first week, so that the analyst will not seem to be cutting off treatment if he or she does not accept the patient.

Once the analyst and patient have settled into analysis, Freud said, the analyst must expect that the patient will be hesitant to discuss two topics: sex and money. Any reduction in the analyst's fees, Freud warned, promotes resistance. It could also jeopardize the analyst's income. When Freud published "On Beginning the Treatment" in 1910, he saw most of his patients six times a week, supporting his family on the fees of just eight people.

Freud emphasized that most of a psychoanalyst's work lies in reacting to a patient's free associations. The interpretation, telling the patient what he or she is really saying, is the psychoanalytic cure. By analyzing the patient's resistance, the analyst reveals the painful compromises the patient has made to hide repressed wishes. Then, by analyzing the patient's transference, the analyst shows the patient the source of those wishes.

This transference is not a sign of mental illness; rather, it shows that the patient and analyst are developing a bond. The secret to free association, after all, is that it is free. The patient can say anything to the analyst, no matter how garbled, shocking, or rude. The analyst, in turn, will not punish the patient or tell her what to do. The patient can say anything she likes. The analyst becomes the vehicle so that the patient's forbidden wishes can come to light. As Freud wrote, "The results of psychoanalysis rest on suggestion . . . true influencing of a person by means of the transference phenomenon."

Freud described three types of transference in his papers "The Dynamics of Transference" and "Observations on Transference Law," published in 1912 and 1914. He stated that negative and erotic transference are fairly easy for a psychoanalyst to define and diagnose. A patient suffering negative transference will be hostile toward the analyst, whereas an erotic transference creates passionate sexual attraction. Both of these states will interfere with the analysis. Hostile patients leave analysis, and erotically interested patients demand the analyst's love. These transferences lead to resistance. Both negative and erotic transference, though, can be stripped away by bringing them to the patient's attention.

The patient then will be left with positive transference. The patient will be ready to work with the analyst as an ally, not as a focus for resistance. As Freud wrote to Jung in 1906, "It is essentially a cure through love." However, Freud expected his analysts not to fall in love with their patients, though their patients frequently fell in love with them. He insisted that a psychoanalyst be aloof and "opaque to his patients and, like a mirror, should show them nothing but what is shown to him." Freud compared psychoanalysts to surgeons, who are emotionally detached, both to protect the analyst and help the patient.

Freud's thinking had changed radically. Instead of curing patients by dredging up memories, suddenly the analyst was curing them through love. Starting with Dora, Freud began to pay more attention to the conflicts patients acted out in analysis. He wrote in 1914, "The patient does not *remember* anything of what he has forgotten and repressed, but *acts* it out. He reproduces it not as a memory but as an action, he *repeats* it without, of course, knowing that he is repeating it." The patient reenacts a situation where his needs were not met, over and over again, because his instinctual desires have not been satisfied. When the patient repeats the situation with an analyst, the patient is guaranteed a sympathetic audience. Yet the analyst is also an authority. By analyzing the transference, the analyst can break the patient's obsession with parents and authority figures. The patient can then become autonomous; he can grow up.

Freud was tired of challenges. His theories had been questioned, the Vienna Psychoanalytic Society was filled with mutineers, and his patients frequently rebelled. In his early days, Freud had been tolerant of his patients' objections and questions. But he now felt that therapists who got their patients to love them would have fewer mutinies.

While Freud was refining his therapeutic techniques, he was also perfecting his theory. The Oedipus complex loomed large in his work as well as in his own life. All of his patients' neuroses, Freud thought, could be traced to the Oedipal family drama, the desire for the parent of the opposite sex and the competition with the same-sex parent. Instead of emphasizing children's ability to find sexual pleasure in many different ways, Freud began to present the Oedipus complex as the only situation that would let children develop into normal adults.

In a 1910 paper entitled "Formulations on the Two Principles of Mental Functioning," Freud translated his ideas

In September 1911, the third International Psychoanalytic Congress was held in Germany. These congresses were forums for discussing current research and were also the scenes of ferocious battles for control of the international psychoanalytic movement.

into more familiar terms. The "primary process," the collection of mental energy, became the "pleasure principle," which seeks satisfaction and is controlled by the "pleasure ego." Secondary processes, which perceive the difference between external and internal events, became "the reality principle," with its own "reality ego." The reality principle protects the pleasure principle by dealing with the real world outside the organism. The pleasure principle is preserved for use at times when pleasure is available—that is, when external circumstances permit.

Freud began to use the term *ego* more often. In 1914, he wrote a paper called "On Narcissism." In Greek mythology, Narcissus was a beautiful young man who fell in love with his own reflection in a pool. Extreme love of the self is normal in children but a sign of illness in adults. Generally, if all of a person's libido, or sexual energy, is attached to another person, the result is infatuation; if it is attached to the self, the result is narcissism. Freud accounted for narcissism in terms of the movement of sexual energy. There can be "ego libido," directed toward the self, he maintained, as well as "object libido," which seeks external sexual pleasure.

This explanation caused Freud trouble. He had previously distinguished between the reality principle and the pleasure principle, and between libido drives and ego drives. Ego drives were supposed to work for self-preserva-tion and be nonsexual; libido drives were sexual. Suddenly, in "On Narcissism," Freud postulated that nonsexual ego drives could be sexual after all. This was a problem. If the ego, the self-preserving secondary process, can be influenced by sex, it would seems that the entire self was motivated only by erotic desires. Though Freud believed that sexual conflicts were at the root of all mental illness, he did not believe that sex was the only motivation in the human mind.

At first, Freud claimed he was simply adding new examples to existing drives. Now there were libidinal drives and nonlibidinal drives, ego-libido, and object-libido, as well as plain old ego. He had started out trying to define the ego in a way that made the concept safe from Adler's wor-rying revisions and "will to power," as well as Jung's asexual libido. Suddenly, Freud's simple two-part scheme of ego and libido was becoming muddled. "On Narcissism" marks the beginning of a new theory of the mind.

In 1915, Freud began work on a book entitled *Introduction to Metapsychology.* He was attempting to rewrite the entire foundation of psychology. In the book, he described the mind from three points of view. First, there were the different parts of the mind: the unconscious repressed urges and memories; the preconscious, which fil-ters materials that can be brought into the conscious mind; and the conscious mind itself. Freud also detailed the move-ment and amount of mental forces and discussed how com-peting drives produce conflict in the unconscious.

In the new book, Freud defined drives as the "demand for work imposed on the mind by its connection with the body." The drives change over time. Love begins in narcis-sism and is transferred to other people by sexual instincts. Hate is the product of a developmental stage earlier than full-blown love, but it is still the result of directing sexual energy at another person. This point contradicted the libido theory and was a sign that further changes were in store.

Freud's definition of repression changed, too. He still believed that the energy connected with a repressed idea is transformed into anxiety. But the thought itself does not disappear. It lurks in the unconscious, ready to turn into fantasies and dreams.

Freud also explained the unconscious. The unconscious contains both repressed thoughts and "primary process" desires, which are not affected by external reality. The unconscious has no sense of time and does not avoid paradoxes or contradictions. It is not subject to the demands and laws of the conscious mind. The preconscious serves as a sort of buffer, where unconscious ideas are put into words and sentences before proceeding to the conscious mind.

One more idea was building in Freud's mind. In his most famous metapsychological essay, "On Mourning and Melancholia" (1917), Freud wrote that the self-punishing thoughts that form melancholic depression are caused by a part of the ego that has become split off from the rest of the ego—it judges and punishes the mourner. This idea of the "split ego" is the first glimmer of Freud's idea of the super-ego, a sort of moral conscience in the psyche.

In all, Freud wrote 12 essays on metapsychology. However, he destroyed seven of them before they could be published. He had changed his mind about the basic concepts he was describing, and about how to fit them into his previous work. Freud was paying attention to the greater human community as well. He published a series of smaller essays about art and culture, including "Leonardo da Vinci and a Memory of His Childhood" (1910) and "The Moses of Michelangelo" (1914). He used these essays to explore the psychoanalytic basis for the artists' work, not only recalling childhood events that influenced their lives but interpreting how they communicated repressed emotions in their art.

In 1913, Freud published a book called *Totem and Taboo,* the first work in which he really applied psychoanalysis to the structures of civilization. Surveying the

On September 14, 1911,
the Freud family gathered
to celebrate Sigmund
and Martha's 25th
wedding anniversary.

On September 14, 1911, the Freud family gathered to celebrate Sigmund and Martha's 25th wedding anniversary.

anthropology current at the time, Freud explained exogamy (marriage outside one's original community), totemism (the worship of and identification with animals or objects), and taboos (rules forbidding certain actions) all through unconscious human desires.

Totem and Taboo includes four essays, but it has one goal: to explain the entire development of human civilization through the Oedipus complex. Once upon a time, Freud wrote, there was a primitive tribe dominated by a violent, sexually possessive father. This father kept all the women for his own sexual use and drove off his sons when they reached sexual maturity. Eventually, these sons banded together and beat him to death. After the father was killed, the sons took the body and ate it, so that each of them would absorb "a piece of his strength." After the crime, though, each brother was overcome by guilt. The sons had loved their father, and after his death they felt his absence keenly. To make up for their evil deeds, the sons now set up a series of taboos— prohibitions against marrying the women of their own tribe, who were now viewed as mothers, wives of the father. The sons were also forbidden to harm the totem. The totem was an animal worshipped as an ancestor of the tribe, but now it was occasionally killed and eaten in a ritual repetition of the brothers' cannibalism. This new state of affairs was the beginning of civilization. As Freud wrote, his story of civilization's development depends on believing that there is a "collective mind" that acts like an individual's mind and that ideas in this "collective mind" can persist for thousands of years. Freud thought that guilt could be inherited.

The idea of a horde of early humans dominated by a powerful male was popular in Freud's time. It was one of Charles Darwin's assumptions when he described human evolution. But by insisting on the reality of the sacrificial meal, Freud took his argument from the realm of psychology and Oedipal fantasy into the world of cultural anthropology. By 1920, anthropologists had published papers observing that most tribes that worship totems do not eat them during sacrificial meals, thus refuting Freud's assertion. Freud also ignored evidence that many people have fantasies of eating their mother. Images of the Earth Mother, who feeds humanity with the milk of her breasts, appear throughout history. Freud ignored the role of women in society in many of his works. The passive, invisible women in *Totem and Taboo* are simply more victims of his neglect.

Freud wrote *Totem* in part as a response to Jung's fascination with mysticism and religion. Jung had noted that psychiatric patients suffering from schizophrenia often had fantasies that resembled the myths of preindustrial tribes. As Freud put it, "In 1912 . . . Jung's forcible indication of the far-reaching analogies between the mental products of neurotics and of primitive peoples led me to turn my attention to that subject." Freud knew that Jung would be disturbed by his paper, but he published it anyway. As he wrote to his colleague Karl Abraham, "Jung is crazy, but I have no desire for a separation and should like to let him wreck himself first. Perhaps my *Totem* paper will hasten the breach against my will." Of course, Freud had other distractions as well. In 1914, Austria-Hungary entered World War I.

Freud in 1916 with two of his sons, Ernst (left) and Martin, who served in the Austrian army. The horrors of World War I spurred Freud to think about the psychological basis of war.

Struggles

Despite the anti-Semitism he had suffered, Freud was a loyal Austro-Hungarian at the start of the war, and he was annoyed when Ernest Jones, an Englishman and psychoanalyst who later wrote a biography of Freud, supported the British cause. (In the war, Germany and Austria-Hungary were opposed by Britain, France, and Russia.) Over time, though, Freud became weary of war. During the war years (1914–18), the psychoanalytic journals Freud had helped to found either stopped publishing or shrank in circulation. The Vienna Psychoanalytic Society had first met every week, then every two weeks, then only occasionally. Freud's three sons joined the army, and his daughter Anna was briefly trapped in England when the fighting started.

Freud began to think about the psychological basis of war. Writing on war and death, he concluded that aggressive impulses are far stronger than society realized. The problem was to sublimate or redirect the energy of this aggression. The war, Freud thought, was the result of a few powerful leaders with bad intentions stirring up their citizens. The people could not truly imagine a war. They thought only of fantasies of honorable battles, where civilians were never killed. Freud did feel that the war would demonstrate to thousands of people that humans were neither basically good nor rational.

People became very interested in psychoanalysis during the war. The reason for this sudden interest was war neurosis, or "shell shock." Thousands of soldiers became psychologically disabled and could not function after experiencing the horrors of the battlefield. Medical authorities were desperate for a method of curing these men. In 1918, representatives from the governments of Germany and the newly separate Austrian and Hungarian republics came to the first international psychoanalytic congress held after the war. But interest in establishing psychological treatment centers for the victims of war neurosis was short-lived because these nations faced internal revolutions.

The years after the war were hard for Freud. There was very little food or fuel in Vienna. Meat and milk disappeared from the Freud household, and pens and paper were scarce from 1918 through 1921. At one point, Freud asked that he be paid in potatoes, not money, for a paper he had written. In the postwar years, Austrian currency underwent incredible inflation. Between 1914 and 1922, the Austrian krone dropped in value by a factor of almost 20,000, falling from 5 to 100,000 kroner to the dollar. Freud responded by writing nagging letters to all of his foreign friends and relatives, requesting food, clothing, and cigars. In Vienna, Freud began to limit his practice to patients from England and the United States who could pay their bills in uninflated currency. Listening to English all day tired Freud, but he enjoyed the financial security. He was able to send regular donations to Lou Andreas-Salomé, one of his favorite psychoanalytic colleagues, throughout the early 1920s. When he discovered she was conducting 10 analyses a day in 1923, he scolded her for overworking herself and sent her more money.

The Viennese also suffered from disease. Epidemics raged, and in 1920 Freud's second daughter, Sophie, died of influenza. Freud was heartbroken, writing to his friend Oskar Pfister, "Sophie leaves two sons of six years and of thirteen months, and an inconsolable husband who will now dearly pay for the happiness of these seven years. That happiness was only between the two of them, not external: war, invasion, being wounded, dwindling away of their possessions, but they had remained brave and cheerful. . . . I work as much as I can, and am thankful for the diversion. The loss of a child seems to be a serious, narcissistic injury; what is known as mourning will probably follow only later."

In the midst of this upheaval, Freud published one of his strangest metapsychological books. Surrounded by the consequences of war and death, he contemplated the human drive for violence. With *Beyond the Pleasure Principle*, published in 1920, Freud added another factor to the psyche already full of drives, repression, the reality principle, and, of course, the pleasure principle. Freud had noticed that there seems to be a "compulsion to repetition." Neurotics have recurring nightmares, and children "act out" frightening scenarios over and over again. In psychoanalysis, the patient reenacts a childhood struggle through transference. Overall, people seem to find themselves in the same situation over and over again.

From this sort of evidence, Freud concluded that human drives were conservative. They are not intended to help the individual develop or grow. Instead, human drives try to recreate the past, to return to previous states. Freud now believed that there were two sets of drives: the libidinal drives, called Eros (after the Greek god of love) and the death instinct, which readers soon called Thanatos (after the Greek god of death). The death instinct is the tendency for life to return to an inanimate state. The instinct for self-preservation, formerly the reality principle, is a part of the death instinct, for it resists death as the result of external causes. It opposes change, so that the organism will die from internal causes instead. Freud wrote, "The aim of all life is death." Even more daring was Freud's declaration that Thanatos included an aggressive drive—the very concept that had led to Adler's expulsion from Freudian society.

Freud made one more key change to his theory. When he created Eros and Thanatos, he abandoned his old energy-based model of the mind. Freud's theory of the psyche was becoming less mechanistic; it no longer called for vaguely biological forces.

Freud's colleagues were not universally pleased with his new work. *Beyond the Pleasure Principle* could have been titled "Beyond Psychoanalysis" from some followers' points of view. The book did not help their practices and did not seem to have any clinical use. It was also difficult to tell if Freud really had discovered a death instinct, or just aggression. Many analysts accepted the idea of conflicting Eros and aggressive instincts and abandoned the rest.

Freud's theory of the psyche was also becoming unwieldy. The concept of Thanatos was difficult to fit into his old division of the conscious, preconscious, and unconscious mind. The death instinct was obviously not part of the conscious or preconscious, or Freud would have noticed it earlier. Yet if both the death instinct and Eros were part of the unconscious, then the unconscious must contain two conflicting drives. If the death instinct was unconscious, it was subject to repression—but by what?

The mind seemed to have more parts than Freud was willing to admit. He saw that the words *conscious* and *unconscious* were becoming confusing; he wanted to replace them with new, more precise terms. Freud redesigned the mind, creating what his followers called the structural theory.

Freud began rebuilding his theory with *The Ego and the Id* (1923). He drew on his experience with resistance. Many patients resist their analysts' efforts without being aware of what they are doing. Therefore the ego, the reality bridge that produces both repression and resistance, cannot be entirely conscious.

Freud now divided the ego. There was a conscious ego, which controlled the motor system (the part of the nervous system that controls movement) and the senses, and an unconscious ego, which repressed upsetting thoughts and censored dreams. Overseeing all of the mind was the superego, which judged and punished. The superego arises out of a child's resolution of the Oedipus complex. The child identifies with the opposite-sex parent and adopts that parent's rules of behavior, especially rules against incest. The id, lurking below, is the source of all desire and instincts and supplies the energy for the unconscious. It contains repressed material, but not everything in the id is repressed. Between the id and the superego sits the reality manager, the ego. The id declares its desires. The ego tries to see what it can do to please the id, but its practical choices are restricted by the superego. The ego simultaneously tries to persuade the id to accept the world's limitations and tries to convince the superego to comply with the id's wishes. In social terms, Freud wrote, the "id is quite amoral, the ego tries to be moral, and the superego can be hyper-moral and cruel."

The superego is not exactly a moral conscience. It absorbs conflicting parental instructions such as "You *ought* to be like your father" and, because the child may not replace the parent, "You *may not be* like your father." The superego can produce unconscious feelings of guilt. These guilt feelings only become obvious in what seem like happy

---

Das Ich und das Es

von

Sigm. Freud

1.—8. Tausend

1923
Internationaler Psychoanalytischer Verlag
Leipzig   Wien   Zürich

In Das Ich und das Es (The Ego and the Id), Freud presented his revolutionary theory that the mind was divided into three separate parts: the ego, the id, and the superego.

circumstances, such as when an analyst congratulates a patient on his or her progress. Sometimes, the patient then becomes much worse, in a "negative therapeutic reaction." Unlike the nightmares he described as defiant acts in *The Interpretation of Dreams*, Freud saw this reaction as a desperate response. The patient's unconscious contains a feeling of guilt, which demands punishment. The superego, perhaps, sometimes serves the death instinct.

The superego was an entirely new concept, but it did not have anywhere near the effect on psychoanalysis as the new improved ego. According to Freud, when an object of love (such as a parent) is lost, that object is replaced in the ego by a representation of that object. In short, parents can continue to affect a child as a representation within the child's ego, as well as through the superego. The question of identification and the ego would soon loom large for Freud and his theories of female development.

Instead of simply repressing the id's desires, the ego was humanity's only hope of balancing the conflicting demands of reality, the id, and the superego. This new role for the ego started the field of ego psychology, the branch of psychoanalytic theory that studies how the ego develops mechanisms for coping with conflicts. In short, this ego psychology allowed Freud and his followers to begin focusing on how a *healthy* ego behaves, instead of focusing on neurotic behavior.

It was also a way to claim ideas from Freud's unfaithful sons Adler and Jung. They had argued that psychoanalysis should not study just symptoms and memory but how the entire personality developed. Ego psychology gave Freud's followers a way of taking over Jung and Adler's views without betraying Freud.

When Freud coined psychological terms, he used German words such as *das Es, das Ich,* and *das Überich,* which translate as the "it," the "I," and the "over-I." Many of the strange, awkward terms in Freudian psychology were

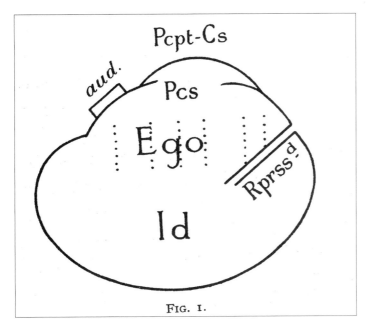

FIG. I.

A diagram from the first English edition of The Ego and the Id shows Freud's conception of the mind's different components.

created by Freud's English-speaking followers, who translated clear, everyday German into Latin *(id, ego, superego)* instead of English. At the time, most medical terms and technical words in other sciences were translated into Latin, and Latin was required in all high schools. Changing German to Latin made psychoanalytic writing sound more scientific in English and helped psychoanalysts in the United States seem more respectable.

In two papers written between 1923 and 1925, Freud began to examine female sexuality again. Many analysts, especially Helene Deutsch, Melanie Klein, Karen Horney, and Freud's biographer Ernest Jones were exploring women's sexual development. Clearly, the sexes developed differently. The question was, how did this happen?

Freud introduced the idea of a new human sexual phase, the phallic phase. He asserted that little boys and girls both believe that everyone has a penis. When the boy resolves his Oedipus complex, he is afraid that his father will destroy his penis. This terror ensures that he will construct a strong superego. Girls, on the other hand, are already "castrated." Freud used social factors to explain changes affecting girls. In a paper titled "The Dissolution of the Oedipus Complex" (1924), he wrote that "these changes seem to be the result of upbringing and of intimidation from outside which threatens her with a loss of love." Two years later, Freud made his opinions explicit in his paper "Some Psychical Consequences of the Anatomical Distinction between the Sexes": "One cannot resist the idea that for woman the level of the ethically normal becomes different [from that in men]. . . . She shows less sense of justice than man, less inclination to submission to the great exigencies of life, is more often led in her decisions by tender or hostile feelings." Her Oedipus complex, Freud claimed, ends with a desire to give her father a baby, which she gradually gives up. But perplexing questions remained: Why should girls abandon their mothers at all? Why should they start to love their fathers?

Here, Freud introduced one of his most notorious concepts: penis envy. When girls see that they do not have their brothers' cherished penises, they begin to feel inferior. Girls then reject their mothers, who may have taken their penises away or at least allowed their daughters to be born inferior. Then the girls become smitten with the penis-bearing father. As Freud wrote, "While the Oedipus complex of the boy is destroyed by the castration complex, that of the girl is made possible and introduced by the castration complex."

Freud's followers, especially Ernest Jones and the small group of female analysts who had gathered around him, were not entirely convinced. As Helene Deutsch later wrote, "it seems unlikely that a trauma of external and accidental origin [noticing one's lack of a penis] should play a fundamental part in the formation of feminine personality." Karen Horney, a German psychoanalyst, read a paper at the 1922 Berlin International Psychoanalytic Congress in which she stated that it might be a "masculine narcissism" of psychoanalysts to assume that women do not wish to be female.

Horney went on to state in a series of papers that the "primal feminine phantasy" is to be raped by the father and have a baby by the father, not to possess a penis. Melanie Klein and Ernest Jones both believed that in girls the phallic phase is not a normal part of development but a neurotic symptom. Girls desired the father's penis and came to hate their mothers because they were rivals, not because they were castrated.

Freud was soon distracted from the debate. In August 1922, his niece, Caecilie Graf, committed suicide. She was pregnant and unmarried, and she died of a drug overdose. Her death shook Freud, as did the death of his late daughter Sophie's son Heinele less than a year later. In February 1923, Freud began an ordeal that would last the rest of his life. He was diagnosed with cancer.

After enduring dozens of years of cigar smoking, Freud's body rebelled. He developed a painful swelling on the roof of his mouth and guessed that it was a malignant tumor. When he consulted his personal physician, though, Freud made the mistake of asking the physician to help him "disappear from the world with decency" if he were suffering needlessly. Freud's doctor took this request as a suicide threat, and only told him that he should have the growth removed, and stop smoking. In fact, Freud had cancer. Freud then consulted a nasal specialist, not an oral surgeon, as would be logical, and was treated incompetently. Freud's colleagues also failed to tell him the truth. Freud was not informed of his diagnosis until September, after he had taken a vacation in Rome with his daughter Anna. Freud had the cancerous growth removed and was fitted with a prosthesis, an artificial jaw plate, so that he could eat and talk again.

In all, Freud had more than 30 operations, not to mention prosthetic fittings and cleanings, over the next 16 years. Yet he did not stop smoking cigars. In 1897, he had written to Fliess that all addictions were substitutes for

Freud with his daughter Anna and an unidentified child. Anna Freud devoted her life to her father and to his work, becoming a renowned psychoanalyst in her own right.

masturbation. Freud knew that he was addicted to cigars, but his self-analysis did not help him to quit. Even when the rational mind knows there is a problem, the unconscious can still hold sway.

Fortunately, Freud had a stalwart source of support through all his trials. His youngest daughter, Anna, had decided to devote her life to her father. Anna Freud had trained as a teacher, and for some time she taught at a girls' school. In 1916, when she was 21, she attended Freud's introductory lectures on psychoanalysis and decided to become an analyst. She told her father that she wished to attend medical school and become a doctor, but he persuaded her to become a lay analyst, without formal medical training. In 1918, he took her into analysis.

Freud had warned his followers against analyzing close friends and associates. How could Freud be neutral toward his daughter? How could he help her win independence from repressed conflicts with her parents through transference? Transferring libido to him would simply transfer it back to her own father, deepening the conflict. After World War I, most students of psychoanalysis began to undergo training analysis to understand themselves and to see what an analysis was like from the patient's point of view. Anna would have to go through one too, if she were to become an analyst. Perhaps Freud worried that his daughter's fantasies and unconscious desires would be too embarrassing to be revealed to other psychoanalysts.

Anna Freud's attachment to her father was unusually strong. She was the one Freud child who decided to enter the family business. Anna had dreams that her father was a king and she a princess, and that people were trying to separate her from her father. When Freud grew ill, Anna, not her mother, became his chief nurse, sleeping in his hospital room and fitting in his jaw prosthesis. Freud, for his part, warned off at least one of Anna's suitors (Ernest Jones) when she was 19, claiming that Anna was "still far away from sexual longing." Jones wrote a perceptive letter to Freud in 1914, saying that Anna "will surely be a remarkable woman later on, provided that her sexual repression does not influence her. She is of course tremendously bound to you."

However "bound" poor Anna may have been, she soon attained high rank in psychoanalytic circles. In 1922, Anna Freud presented to the Vienna Psychoanalytic Society a scientific paper on masturbatory fantasies of being beaten, and she was soon made a full member of the society. Over time, Anna began to represent her father at international congresses when he felt he could not travel. Freud continued to fret over Anna's lack of female friends, and Anna worried about her father's digestion. His daughter's continuing emotional dependence concerned Freud, but he did not know how to end it and probably did not wish to do so. Having encouraged Anna to become an analyst, Freud was honor bound to defend her choice.

In the early 1920s, Freud's fame was spreading rapidly. Before World War I, most psychoanalysts had been personally trained by Freud or one of his close associates. Now there were psychoanalytic institutes in New York and London. How could the International Psychoanalytic Association make sure that its standards and principles were maintained? This question was especially important in the English-speaking countries. Self-styled "analysts" with no training were hanging out shingles everywhere. Medical and academic professionals in the United States were making remarks like those of M. McKeen Cattell, president of the American Association for the Advancement of Science, who said that psychoanalysis was "not so much a question of science as a matter of taste, Dr. Freud being an artist who lives in the fairyland of dreams among the ogres of perverted sex."

It was in this environment that Freud wrote *The Question of Lay Analysis* (1926). Freud strongly supported lay analysis, his daughter's profession. He wrote to a friend, "I want to protect analysis from the doctors." Freud claimed that he lacked the proper "medical disposition," and that a medical degree was not only unnecessary for analysis but that doctors were sadly prejudiced. Writing in October 1927, Freud declared, "The physicians among the analysts have only been too inclined to engage in research closer to the organic, rather than in psychological research."

However, Freud was not the emperor of psychoanalysis he had once been. The New York Psychoanalytic Society continued to require a medical degree for psychoanalytic training. Its position was that it was politically and financially desirable to have only medical professionals conduct psychoanalysis and charge high fees. Even Caroline Newton, who had been in analysis with Freud and translated Otto Rank's writings into English, was refused admission into the society. The American refusal to train lay analysts did have the effect of excluding women from the profession in the

United States. By contrast, the British Psychoanalytic Society trained lay analysts, and in the 1920s about 40 percent of England's analysts were not physicians. Elsewhere, the Hungarian Psychoanalytic Society supported Freud, while the Viennese continued to argue.

By 1929, Abraham Brill, head of the New York Psychoanalytic Society, was nervous about the society's drift away from Freud. Leery of beginning his own psychoanalytic movement, Brill agreed to allow some lay people to begin psychoanalytic training. Even the Americans had to admit that psychoanalysis had no connection to medical biology in the end.

Exhaustion

Freud was becoming a celebrity, especially in America. In 1924, the *Chicago Tribune* offered him $25,000 to analyze Nathan Leopold and Richard Loeb, who as college students set out to commit "the perfect crime" and kidnapped and murdered a 15-year-old boy in Chicago. That same year, the Hollywood producer Samuel Goldwyn offered Freud $100,000 to consult on a love story for the silver screen, calling Freud "the greatest love specialist in the world." He refused both offers.

Freud was increasingly concerned with how to apply psychoanalysis to society. As he wrote in his 1925 *Autobiographical Study,* "I perceived ever more clearly that the events of human history, the interactions between human nature, cultural development and the precipitates of primeval experience (the most prominent of which is religion) are no more than a reflection of the dynamic conflicts between the ego, the id, and the super-ego, which psychoanalysis studies in the individual—are the very same processes repeated upon a wider stage."

In 1927, Freud published *The Future of an Illusion*, an investigation of the origins of religion. Freud begins the

Freud relaxes in 1932 at a farmhouse outside of Vienna owned by his daughter Anna. By this time, Freud was in great pain, tormented by an artificial jaw he had received after surgery to remove a cancerous growth in his jaw.

book by discussing the relationship between society and the individual. Culture, according to Freud, exists to "control the forces of nature" and to "adjust the relations of men to one another." Individuals must be forced to suppress their desires for the sake of the community. Yet humans are helpless in the face of nature's floods, earthquakes, and epidemics. Freud saw that humans' relationship to nature was like a child's relationship to its parents. Children live at the mercy of their powerful parents, whom they need to protect them. When children grow up, they transfer their parental ties to gods to satisfy the same infantile needs the parents filled when the believer was young. Religion, in short, is an illusion expressing the wish for eternal parental protection.

Freud claimed that religion did not make the devout happy or help people adapt to civilization. He stated, "an appallingly large number of people are dissatisfied with civilization and unhappy with it, and feel it as a yoke which must be shaken off." By contrast, Freud wrote, "The scientific spirit brings about a particular attitude towards worldly matters. . . . The greater the number of men to whom the treasures of knowledge become accessible, the more widespread is the falling away from religious belief."

Freud once again attracted attention in the United States, inspiring headlines like "Religion Doomed Freud Asserts" in the *New York Times* in December 1927. Theologians denounced the book, and Oskar Pfister, a Protestant pastor and personal friend of Freud's, wrote a polite rebuttal titled "The Illusion of a Future." Anti-Semites denounced Freud for trying to destroy the Christian religion. Everyone accused Freud of trying to undermine public morality, first with his theories about sex, now through denying God.

Meanwhile, Freud's jaw prosthesis tormented him. He frequently had difficulty speaking and eating and was often in pain. One of Freud's young students, Maryse Choisy, remembers Freud saying of *The Future of an Illusion,* "This is my worst book! . . . It isn't a book of Freud. . . . It's the book of an old man! Besides Freud is dead now, and believe me, the genuine Freud was really a great man. I am particularly sorry for you that you didn't know him better." After he contracted cancer Freud stopped writing case histories and concentrated solely on larger philosophical issues of psychoanalysis and culture. He cut his caseload drastically, abandoning mere human relationships and withdrawing into impersonal scholarly writing. He had almost stopped treating people, except as abstractions.

Though Freud's body was a prisoner of cancer, he began work on a new book, *Civilization and its Discontents,* which was published in 1930. Like *The Future of an Illusion, Civilization* described the interaction of the individual, religion, and culture. Freud started with the assumption that humans are unhappy. When we are not threatened by storms, earthquakes, and plagues, he wrote, we are watching our bodies crumbling, waiting for death. We distract ourselves, Freud continued, in different ways. One distraction is religion. Another is work. Yet all of these activities fail us in the end. When people are unhappy, they become hostile to civilization. Freud cited modern resistance to science as just one example of this hostility. Technical advances could not bring happiness. Humans were too cruel to each other. Civilization's major contribution to human happiness is to protect people from their neighbors' bad intentions. Civilization, Freud claimed, keeps humans from killing each other.

By now, Freud had accepted the aggressive drive as a part of the human psyche. Aggression, Freud wrote, was not only a drive but a pleasure that was hard to give up once enjoyed. It also helped to bind a group together. Members of a group are closer when there is some other group they can hate. After all, love is exclusive, according to Freud. It is an enemy to civilization. On the other hand, civilization also undermines love by hobbling it with laws and taboos.

Civilization enforces its laws by acting as a sort of "cultural superego." As a child develops a superego by internalizing his father's standards of conduct, so a member of a culture will absorb his society's taboos. However, just as humans develop neuroses when there are struggles between the superego and the id's demands, cultures can become mentally ill. Freud pointed to the ancient Israelites, who punished themselves for their sinfulness by creating a strict, inflexible religion with self-accusing prophets and severe laws.

One symptom sums up humans' relationship to their civilization: guilt. Society helps ensure human survival, but only at the cost of forcing individuals to betray their instincts. Guilt is an expression of anxiety created by this compromise. Civilization ensures that humans will always be discontented.

In 1930 Freud won the Goethe Prize, an award presented by the city of Frankfurt, Germany, to those who had made great contributions to culture. Freud was especially pleased with the 10,000 deutsche mark stipend attached to the prize. But Freud had to send his daughter Anna to the ceremony because he was too ill to attend. At 74, Freud was an old, sick man. His oral surgeon continually checked for recurrences of cancer, and Freud even gave up his beloved cigars.

The same year, Freud's mother died, at the age of 95. Freud was not shaken, as he was after his father's death. Instead, he felt relief; relief that his mother was free from suffering and relief that he, too, could die without causing her suffering. Freud wrote to Ernest Jones that he felt a "growth in personal freedom" since "it was always an abhorrent thought that she [Amalia] would learn of my death." Though Freud may have felt free, he was more limited than ever before. Another jaw operation in 1931 left him too weak to travel back to his birthplace, where, with great ceremony, a commemorative plaque was placed on the house where he was born.

In 1931, the Great Depression paralyzed Europe. Nevertheless, on income from awards, book royalties, and part-time analysis, Freud managed to support both his family and his sons-in-law. Economic hardships in Germany and Austria made ordinary people desperate for any possible solution, and Adolf Hitler was appointed chancellor of Germany in 1933. Within six months, his Nazi party organized nationwide book burnings of works by Jews, democrats, and leftists, including the books of Albert Einstein, Franz Kafka, Thomas Mann, and Freud himself.

Vienna's slow slide into dictatorship did not move Freud to leave the country. Friends abroad, more perceptive than Freud, began to send him offers of asylum, but Freud resisted. He was comfortable in Vienna. He had lived in the same house for nearly 40 years and had friends and relatives who cared for him.

Freud was also tired. In 1937, he published an essay titled "Analysis Terminable and Interminable," a rethinking

Nazi officers in Germany round up a group of Jews for transportation to a concentration camp. Freud's friends and colleagues in Austria were troubled by the rise of the Nazis in Germany and encouraged Freud to flee.

of psychoanalytic therapy. Freud had come to believe that psychoanalysis was a weak weapon compared to the strength of the psychic drives, especially the death drive. Not only was psychoanalysis unable to cure some patients, but many patients who underwent successful analysis had to return for more sessions after a relapse. Some patients needed to attend psychoanalytic sessions through their entire lives. In the end, Freud viewed psychoanalysis not primarily as a therapy but as a method of research. He became more interested in discovering the deep motivations that underlie human behavior and the rules of civilization, rather than curing a single person's woes.

While Freud was questioning the very therapy he had created, Austria was collapsing. Freud's more politically astute pupils saw that sooner or later the Nazis would take over the country. Throughout the 1930s, they fled, leaving Freud more and more isolated. This dispersal frightened Freud. Who would be left in Vienna to protect psychoanalysis, if he did not stay? Now the psychoanalysts, like the Jews, became a diaspora: scattered around the world, with no real home. Herman Nunberg, one of the young analysts who left Austria, remembers Freud telling him "that there was no real danger, that the existing government of Austria would protect the Jews and not yield to the Nazis. As for him, he said, he was an old man and a sick one; Vienna was his home, and it was there that his doctors were, men who knew him well and whom he needed."

On March 11, 1938, the Austrian chancellor allowed German troops to cross the border and annex Austria. Almost immediately, Austrian mobs began looting Jewish stores and apartments and beating Jews on the street. The Nazis quickly came to search both Freud's home and the Viennese psychoanalytic publishing house, taking money and whatever papers they could find. Martin Freud remembered his mother, ever the guardian of an orderly household, reacting during one raid: "The . . . scene . . . is of mother, highly indignant with an SS man who, on his way through a passage, paused at a large cupboard, pulled open its doors and began roughly dragging out her piles of beautifully laundered linen all efficiently arranged in the way dear to her housewifely heart, each package held together by colored ribbons. Without showing the slightest fear, mother joined the fellow and in highly indignant tones told him precisely what she thought of his shocking behavior in a lady's house, and ordered him to stop at once. The SS man, a big fellow, jumped back from the cupboard and looked quite terrified, quickly withdrawing and appearing very sheepish indeed as mother rearranged her linen."

Freud was still reluctant to leave. He was old, he was weak, and he was afraid that he would not be accepted by any other country. In 1938, the world was not sympathetic to Jewish refugees. Ernest Jones flew to Vienna to persuade Freud to leave, and finally convinced him that though he might be abandoning Austria, Austria had already abandoned him. Though the new Nazi government was reluctant to let Freud leave the country, he had powerful friends in the international community. The U.S. ambassador to France, the U.S. consul general in Vienna, the Princess Marie Bonaparte—who was related to most of the crowned heads of Europe—and Ernest Jones's friends in the British Foreign Office worked madly to get Freud to England. Anna was arrested by the Gestapo but kept her wits about her and was released. The Nazis demanded money to let Freud go, which Marie Bonaparte paid. Freud was allowed to leave Vienna on June 4, 1938. He would never return. Although he managed to save most of his family members still living in Vienna, he had to leave behind his four sisters. One starved to death in the Theresienstadt concentration camp; the other three probably died at Auschwitz.

Freud arrived in London on June 6, 1938, and a few months later settled in a rented house in Maresfield Gardens, a London suburb. Eventually, Freud's couch,

Freud and Anna finally left Austria on June 4, 1938. The new Nazi government was reluctant to let Freud leave but bowed to pressure from the international community.

books, and collections were ransomed from the Nazis and delivered to England. Martha and the Freuds' housekeeper managed to arrange Freud's beloved statues on Freud's new desk exactly the same way he had kept them in Vienna. In fact, the entire house was arranged as a near replica of Freud's chambers at Berggasse 19, and Freud was soon analyzing a few patients. Yet he was still pensive. When a visitor mentioned that his new study was identical to his old one in Vienna, Freud replied wearily, "Everything is here, only I am not here."

Freud's final book was *Moses and Monotheism*, and it was one of his most controversial works. It was not strictly a book on psychoanalytic theory. Freud himself referred to it as his "historical novel." With *Moses,* Freud returned to the topic of Judaism. He had been fascinated with Moses for years and had written an essay on Michelangelos's statue of the great biblical figure. The book consists of three essays with one theme: that Moses, who led the ancient Israelites out of slavery in Egypt, was himself an Egyptian nobleman. Moses embraced monotheism, the belief that there is just one god, at a time when most Egyptians belonged to pagan cults. He converted the Jews to monotheism and brought them out of Egypt into the Holy Land. There the Hebrews met a tribe called the Midianites who worshipped a god named Yahweh, a vengeful god. The Jews then rebelled against Moses and killed him. The revolt against Moses, Freud claimed, was a reenactment of the original ancient murder of the father. Given that Judaism began with a return to repressed primal experience, Christianity probably disguised a primal act as well. Jesus, too, was most likely the leader of a band of brothers who had killed their father long ago.

With some misgivings, Freud published the book. He worried about the reception of his work in the Jewish community. He wrote in a letter to the historian Charles Singer, "Needless to say, I don't like offending my own people. . . . But what can I do about it? I have spent my whole life standing up for what I have considered to be the scientific truth, even when it was uncomfortable and unpleasant for my fellow men. I cannot end up with an act of disavowal."

As he had anticipated, Freud was widely criticized for *Moses and Monotheism.* Opponents called his writing historically inaccurate and his conclusions offensive. Yet the book sold well and was quickly translated into English. It was fortunate that this was done quickly. Freud was dying. His cancer had recurred in the fall of 1937, and he could no longer stand surgical treatments. In February 1939, his new London doctors declared his cancer incurable and

Freud in the study of his London home in 1938, a year before his death.

inoperable. In July, he stopped seeing patients but continued to read. The last book he read was a novel by Balzac, the same author he had forbidden his sister to read many years earlier.

The cancerous tissue began to ulcerate and produce a horrible smell. From August onward, Freud's dog refused to go near him. The dying man had begun yet another revision of his theory, titled "Outline of Psychoanalysis," but he abandoned it, partly because he was in constant pain. He refused to take medication, though, because he wanted to keep his mind sharp. On September 21, 1939, Freud asked Max Schur, his personal physician, to help him, saying, "Now it is nothing but torture and makes no sense." After consulting with Anna, Schur injected Freud with an overdose of morphine. Over the next two days, he gave Freud two more injections. On September 23, 1939, Dr. Sigmund Freud, the founder of psychoanalysis, was dead. Contrary to Jewish custom, his body was cremated, and his ashes were placed in his favorite Grecian urn. And loyal Martha Bernays Freud, for the first time since her marriage, lit the Jewish Sabbath candles on Friday night.

Epilogue

Confronted by a human being who impresses us as great, should we not be moved rather than chilled by the knowledge that he might have attained his greatness only through his frailties?
—Lou Andreas-Salomé, *Freud Journal* (1964)

Freud's work was not perfect. He did not tolerate doubters, and he tossed some of his most talented students out of his movement on the grounds that they did not show enough respect for his ideas. Both the topics of his research and his methods for reaching his conclusions have remained controversial to this day. Though many current literary critics cite *The Interpretation of Dreams* to support their theories, some biologists object that Freud's conception of the human mind is an utter fraud, not even worthy of study. In 1995, an exhibit on Freud scheduled to open at the U.S. Library of Congress had to be postponed partly because the curator could not find a way to please both the pro- and anti- Freudians.

This is the paradox: Freud inspires both intense loyalty and fierce hatred. His close analysis of human behavior and

As this drawing from 1970 suggests, Freud's life and work continue to be the subject of controversy. Are Freud's ideas simply the product of his own imagination and circumstances or do they offer the world a new way to explore the mind?

its relationship to underlying mental conflicts gave anthropology, history, literary theory, and dozens of other disciplines valuable tools for analyzing human life and art. In particular, Freud paid close attention to language, and his theories of dreams and "slips" (customarily referred to as "Freudian slips") have given students of literature a rich new way of understanding the written word.

At the same time, Freud's work infuriates many scientists, psychologists, and feminist authors. His research methods were very different from those used in most other scientific work, and his belief that much of behavior is determined by early childhood experiences looks like a way to help adults avoid taking responsibility for their actions. Some of Freud's theories of women's psychology are, in fact, hurtful to women, and encourage therapists to view women as weak and immature. Even more damaging, some people feel, is that structures like the id or the ego cannot be detected except by Freud's techniques. There is no way to scan a brain to find a superego. The only way to find it is to deduce that the superego must be there from its effects. For many anti-Freudians, Freud's psychology seems to rely on faith, not on scientific evidence. Max Graf, a member of the Wednesday Psychological Society and the father of "Little Hans," wrote in an article published in *The Psychoanalytic Quarterly* in 1942:

> There was the atmosphere of a religion in that room. Freud himself was its new prophet who made the. . . prevailing methods of psychological investigation appear superficial. Freud's pupils—all inspired and convinced—were his apostles. [a reference to Jesus Christ's first followers] . . . After the first dreamy period and the unquestioning faith of the first group of apostles, the time came when the church was founded. Freud began to organize his church with great energy. He was serious and strict in the demands made of his pupils; he permitted no deviation from his orthodox teachings. . . . If we do consider him as a founder of a religion, we may think of him as Moses full of wrath and unmoved by prayers.

There is no easy resolution to the pro/anti-Freud debate. Freud is as controversial as ever because he is still one of the most influential thinkers of the 20th century. Yet today, Freud would not be able to begin his research. In the 20th century, hysteria disappeared. Fewer and fewer women and men showed hysterical symptoms after 1900, and the American Psychiatric Association no longer lists hysteria as a mental illness. The physical symptoms that Freud recognized as hysterical are now called conversion disorders—where psychological problems are "converted" into physical symptoms—and are not believed to be linked to childhood trauma. The disease that spurred Freud's investigation of the mind no longer officially exists.

Freud's greatest contribution to science was not his treatment for hysteria or neurotic behavior. Freud gave the world a new way to explore the mind. He was not a scientist in the modern sense. But he made it possible for thousands of researchers, therapists, artists, and writers to explore the unconscious motivations behind behavior, the feelings that we will not admit to, the dark foundation below the facade of rational thought.

CHRONOLOGY

May 6, 1856
Born Sigismund Shlomo Freud in Freiberg, Moravia

1860
Freud family moves to Vienna

1873
Freud enters the University of Vienna

1881
Freud receives M.D. degree; works full-time in Ernst Brücke's laboratory

1882
Freud begins work at the General Hospital of Vienna; becomes engaged to Martha Bernays

1884
Freud publishes "On Coca"

1885
Travels to Charcot's clinic in Paris

1886
Lectures on hysteria to Viennese Society of Physicians; sets up own clinic

1887
Matilde Freud born; Freud meets Wilhelm Fliess

1889
Martin Freud born

1891
Oliver Freud born

1892
Ernst Freud born

1893
Sophie Freud born

1895
Freud has "The Dream of Irma's Injection"; publishes *Studies on Hysteria*

1896
Anna Freud born; Freud's father dies; Freud lectures on seduction theory in Vienna

1897
Freud begins self-analysis; rejects seduction theory

1902
Freud stops corresponding with Fliess; Wednesday Psychological Society begins

1904
Freud begins to correspond with Carl Jung

1905
Publishes *Three Essays on the Theory of Sexuality*

1909
Visits the United States

1914
Writes "On Narcissism"; Word War I begins

1918
Representatives from three governments attend first psychoanalytic conference after the war

1920
Freud publishes *Beyond the Pleasure Principle*

1920
Sophie Freud dies

1922
Anna Freud joins Vienna Psychoanalytic Society

1923
Freud is diagnosed with jaw cancer

1926
Publishes "The Question of Lay Analysis"

1929
Writes *Civilization and Its Discontents*

1933
Nazis burn Freud's books in Germany

1938
Freud flees Vienna; publishes *Moses and Monotheism*

September 23, 1939
Dies in England

FURTHER READING

Freud's Life and Times

Anzieu, Didier. *Freud's Self Analysis.* London: Hogarth Press/Institute of Psycho-Analysis, 1986.

Appignanesi, Lisa, and John Forrester. *Freud's Women.* London: Weidenfeld and Nicolson, 1992.

Crews, Frederick. *Skeptical Engagements.* New York: Oxford University Press, 1986.

Diller, Jerry V. *Freud's Jewish Identity: A Case Study in the Impact of Ethnicity.* Madison, N.J.: Fairleigh Dickinson University Press, 1991.

Engelman, Edmund. *Berggasse 19: Sigmund Freud's Home and Offices, Vienna 1938.* New York: Basic Books, 1976.

Freud, Martin. *Sigmund Freud: Man and Father.* New York: Vanguard, 1958.

Gay, Peter. *Freud: A Life for Our Time.* New York: Doubleday, 1988.

Gilman, Sander. *Freud, Race, and Gender.* Princeton, N.J.: Princeton University Press, 1993.

Jones, Ernest. *The Life and Work of Sigmund Freud.* 3 volumes. New York: Basic Books, 1957.

Krull, Marianne. *Freud and His Father.* New York: Norton, 1986.

Rieff, Philip. *Freud: The Mind of the Moralist.* 3rd edition. Chicago: University of Chicago Press, 1979.

Roazen, Paul. *Freud and His Followers.* New York: New York University Press, 1984.

Schorske, Carl E. *Fin-de-Siècle Vienna: Politics and Culture.* New York: Vintage, 1981.

Sulloway, Frank J. *Freud: Biologist of the Mind.* Cambridge: Harvard University Press, 1992.

Selected Writings of Freud

Freud, Sigmund. *The Basic Writings of Sigmund Freud.* New York: Random House, 1995.

———. *Civilization and Its Discontents.* 1927. Reprint, New York: Norton, 1989.

———. *The Complete Letters of Sigmund Freud to Wilhelm Fliess, 1887–1904.* Edited by Jeffrey Moussaieff Masson. Cambridge: Harvard University Press, 1985.

————. *The Ego and the Id*. 1923. Reprint, New York: Norton, 1990.

————. *The Interpretation of Dreams*. 1900. Reprint, New York: Random House, 1996.

————. *Letters of Sigmund Freud*. Edited by Ernst Freud. Translated by Tania Stern and James Stern. New York: Basic Books, 1960.

————. *Moses and Monotheism*. 1939. Reprint, New York: Random House, 1955.

————. *New Introductory Lectures on Psychoanalysis*. 1933. Reprint, New York: Norton, 1990.

————. *Totem and Taboo*. 1913. Reprint, New York: Norton, 1990.

The History of Psychoanalysis

Appignanesi, Richard. *Freud for Beginners*. New York: McKay, 1990.

Ellenberger, Henri. *The Discovery of the Unconscious: The History and Evolution of Dynamic Psychiatry*. New York: Basic Books, 1970.

Gay, Peter. *Reading Freud: Explorations and Entertainments*. New Haven: Yale University Press, 1990.

Gelfand, Toby, and John Kerr, eds. *Freud and the History of Psychoanalysis*. Hillsdale, N.J.: Analytic Press, 1992.

Hale, Nathan G. *Freud and the Americans: The Origin and Foundation of the Psychoanalytic Movement in America*. New York: Oxford University Press, 1971.

————. *The Rise and Crisis of Psychoanalysis in the United States: Freud and the Americans, 1917–1985*. New York: Oxford University Press, 1996.

Horowitz, Mardi J., ed. *Hysterical Personality*. New York: Aronson, 1977.

Macmillan, Malcolm. *Freud Evaluated: The Completed Arc*. New York: North-Holland, 1991.

Stwertka, Eve. *Psychoanalysis: From Freud to the Age of Therapy*. New York: Watts, 1988.

INDEX

Page numbers in *italics* indicate illustrations.

Abraham, Karl, 119
Adler, Alfred, *107*-9, 116, 126
American Psychiatric
  Association, 149
"Analysis Terminable and
  Interminable" (Freud), 140
Andreas-Salomé, Lou, 122,
  147
Anna O. (patient), 45, 50-53,
  60, 62, 69-70
Anti-Semitism, 12, 13, 14, 15-
  17, 88, 99, 136, *139*-41
Austria, 15-17, 139-41. *See
  also* Vienna
Autobiographical Study (Freud),
  134

Balzac, Honoré de, 20, 144
Bauer, Ida. *See* Dora
Bernays, Eli, 26, 27
Bernays, Jacob, 52
Bernays, Minna, 28, 68
Bernheim, Hippolyte, 50, 57-
  58
Beyond the Pleasure Principle
  (Freud), 123, 124
Bisexuality, 54, 56, 92, 98-99,
  102-3
Bleuler, Eugene, 99
B'nai B'rith, 81
Bonaparte, Princess Marie,
  141
Brentano, Franz, 22-23, 24, 44
Breuer, Josef, 44-45, 50-53,
  58, 59, 60-61, 69-70
Brill, Abraham, 133
Briquet, Paul, 34-35
British Psychoanalytic
  Society, 133

Brücke, Ernst, *23*-25, 32, 67,
  70

Catharsis, 52, 53, 57, 70
Cattell, M. McKeen, 132
Charcot, Jean-Martin, 32, *34*-
  40, 45-46, 48-49, 54, 59, 67
Choisy, Maryse, 136-37
Civilization and Its Discontents
  (Freud), 107
Clark University, 105-6
Cocaine, 30-32, *33*
Conversion disorder, 149
Countertransference, 98
Cromwell, Oliver, 67

Darwin, Charles, 21-*22*, 119
Deutsch, Helene, 127, 128
"Dissolution of the Oedipus
  Complex, The" (Freud), 128
Dora (patient), 98-99, 102
"Dynamics of Transference,
  The" (Freud), 113

Eckstein, Emma, 75-77
Ego, 72, 115-17, 125-27
Ego and the Id, The (Freud),
  124-*27*
Elisabeth von R. (patient), 58,
  60
Emmy von N. (patient), 57-58
Epilepsy, 32, 35
Eros, 123-24

Faradization, *47*
Ferenczi, Sándor, 99, 105,
  106, 109
Feuerbach, Ludwig, 22
Fleischl-Markow, Ernst von,
  31-32
Fliess, Wilhelm, 53, 54-57, 64,
  68, 70, 72-73, 76-78

"Formulations on the Two
  Principles of Mental
  Functioning" (Freud), 114-
  15
Franz Josef (emperor), 16
Free association, 58
Freud, Adolfine (sister), 12
Freud, Alexander (brother), 12
Freud, Amalia (mother), 11,
  12, *13*, 14, 18-19, 68, 138
Freud, Anna (daughter), 67,
  86, 96, 121, 129, 130-31,
  138, 141, 144
Freud, Anna (sister), 12, 19,
  20, 26
Freud, Emanuel (half-brother), 13, 14, 18
Freud, Ernst (son), 67
Freudian slips, 82-83, 86, 148
Freud, Jacob (father), 11, 12-
  14, 18-19, 78-79
Freud, Jean Martin (son), 27,
  67, 68, 140
Freud, Josef (uncle), 14
Freud, Julius (brother), 19
Freud, Marie (sister), 12
Freud, Martha Bernays (wife),
  25, 26-29, 31, *42*, 57, 67-68,
  140-41, 142, 145
Freud, Matilde (daughter), 44,
  68-69
Freud, Oliver (son), 67
Freud, Pauline (sister), 12
Freud, Philipp (half-brother),
  13, 14, 18-19
Freud, Rosa (sister), 12
Freud, Sigmund
  analysis of daughter by, 130-
    31
  atheism of, 17, 22, 29
  biases of, 74-75
  birth of, 11

cancer of, 129-30, 136-37,
  143-44
case studies of, 62-64, 96-
  102. See also specific cases
and cathartic technique, 57,
  70
childhood of, 11-14, 15
children of, 44, 66-69, 123
as clinician, 43-44, 68
cocaine research of, 30-32,
  33
courtship of wife by, 25, 27-
  29, 31, 42
criticisms of, 111-12, 148-
  49
Darwin's influence on, 21-
  22, 119
death of, 143-45
death of father of, 78-79,
  82, 87
dreams of, 77-78, 84
dream theories of, 84-87
and drives, 123-24
education of, 20-24
engagement of, 25
family of, 11, 12-13, 18-19,
  44, 66-69, 123. See also
  individual family members
fascination with Moses of,
  13, 117, 143
father figures of, 23, 44-45,
  87, 98-99
and free association, 58, 65,
  70, 96-97, 112-12
friendship with Fliess of, 53,
  54-57, 64, 68, 70, 72-73,
  76-78, 87, 90-92, 98-99
home life of, 67-69, 95-96
and homosexuality, 98-99,
  102-3
use of hypnosis by, 48, 50,
  59-60
and hysteria, 38-39, 45-46,
  48, 50, 52-53, 58-61, 94
immigration to London of,
  141-42
as a Jew, 13-14, 16, 17-18,
  81

lecture to Society of
  Physicians by, 45-46
metapsychological views of,
  116-19, 123, 137-38
military service of, 24
modern view of, 10-11,
  148-49
and neuroses, 73, 84
nursemaid of, 19, 83
and obsessions, 74-75, 94,
  99-101
and Oedipus complex, 83
office of, 8-10, 96, 105, 142
and phobias, 96, 101-2
process of analysis as viewed
  by, 112-14
as professor, 88-89
religious views of, 134-36,
  142-43
and repression, 71-72, 73-75
and seduction theory, 74-
  75, 81-82
self-psychoanalysis of, 82-
  83, 87
and sexual development
  states, 93-95, 109-10
and structural theory, 124-
  27
as teaching assistant, 24-25
and telepathy, 54
theory of the unconscious
  by, 86-87, 117
as translator, 24, 38, 49
view of lay analysts of, 132
views of aggression of, 121-
  22, 137-38
views of women's sexuality
  by, 74-756, 95, 102-3, 119,
  127-29
visit to Rome by, 87-88
visit to U.S. by, 104-6
wedding of, 44
Freud, Sophie (daughter), 67,
  123
Future of an Illusion, The
  (Freud), 22, 134-36

Goldwyn, Samuel, 134
Graf, Caecilie, 129
Graf, Max, 101-2, 147

Hall, G. Stanley, 105, 106
Heine, Heinrich, 107
Hippocrates, 33
History of the Psychoanalytic
  Movement (Freud), 111
Hofmannsthal, Hugo von, 20
Homosexuality, 98-99, 102-3
Horney, Karen, 127, 128-29
Hungarian Psychoanalytic
  Society, 133
Hydrotherapy, 47
Hypnotism, 32, 35, 36, 37,
  39-41, 46, 48-50
Hysteria
  Charcot's work with, 34-39
  Freud's experience with, 46,
    48, 50, 53-53, 58-61
  history of, 32-34
  modern view of, 149
  as result of frustrated sexual-
    ity, 33-34, 58-61, 69, 71-
    72 74-75, 81-82
  seizures during, 35
  treatment of, 34
Hysterical paralysis, 36

Id, 125-27
Individual psychology, 109
International Psychoanalytic
  Association, 106-7, 110-11
Interpretation of Dreams, The
  (Freud), 22, 79, 85, 86, 87,
  88, 90, 93, 126, 148
Introduction to Metapsychology
  (Freud), 116-17

James, William, 106
Janet, Pierre, 65
Jews, Austrian, 15-17, 18, 88,
  99, 136, 139-41. See also
  Anti-Semitism
Jones, Ernest, 99, 109, 121,
  127, 128, 129, 131, 138, 141

Jung, Carl, 99, 105, 106, *109-11*, 119, 126

Katharina R. (patient), 62, 63
Klein, Melanie, 127, 129
Klimt, Gustav, 20
Koller, Carl, 31
Königston, Leopold, 31, 68
Krafft-Ebing, Richard von, 75

Lay analysts, 132-33
Leonardo da Vinci, 87
Leopold, Nathan, 134
Libido, 85, 95, 108, 109
Library of Congress (U.S.), 148
Little Hans (patient), 101-2
Loeb, Richard, 134
Lueger, Karl, 88

Mahler, Gustav, 20
Mesmerism, 40-*41*, 52. *See also* Hypnotism
Meynert, Theodor, 49
Michelangelo, 87
Mill, John Stuart, 24
Moses, 13, 142-43
Moses and Monotheism (Freud), 142-43
"Moses of Michelangelo, The" (Freud), 117

Nasal-genital theory, 54-56
Nazis, 12, 18, 67, *139*, 140-41
Neurosis, 73, 84
Newton, Caroline, 132
Newton, Isaac, 73
New York Psychoanalytic Society, 132
Nothnagel, Hermann, 44
Nunberg, Herman, 140

"Observation on Transference Law" (Freud), 113
Obsessions, 74-75, 94, 99-101
Oedipus complex, 83, 86, 103, 14, 118, 125, 127-28

"On Beginning Treatment" (Freud), 112
"On Mourning and Melancholia" (Freud), 117
"On Narcissism" (Freud), 115-16

Pappenheim, Bertha. *See* Anna O.
Pasteur, Louis, 36
Penis envy, 128
Periodicity, 54, 56, 90
Pfister, Oskar, 123, 136
Phobias, 96, 101-2
Pinel, Philippe, 33
Project for a Scientific Psychology (Freud), 70-73, 77, 78
Psychoanalysis, derivation of name, 65
Psychoanalytic institutes, 132-33
Psychopathology of Everyday Life, The (Freud), 69
Putnam, James, 106

Question of Lay Analysis, The (Freud), 132

Rank, Otto, 93, 109, 132
Rat Man (patient), 99-101
Repression, 71-72, 73-75

Sachs, Hanns, 105, 108
Salpêtrière Hospital (Paris), 32, 36, *38*
Schnitzler, Arthur, 20
Schoenberg, Arnold, 20
Schur, Max, 144-45
Seduction theory, 74-75, 81-82
Sexual trauma, 63, 74-75
Shell shock, 122
Singer, Charles, 143
Society for Free Psycho-analysis (Vienna), 108
Society of Physicians (Vienna), 45-46

"Some Psychical Consequences of the Anatomical Distinction between the Sexes" (Freud), 128
Stekel, Wilhelm, 92
Studies on Hysteria (Freud), 58, 60, 69, 70, 88
Superego, 117, 125-27
Swoboda, Hermann, 92
Sydenham, Thomas, 33

Talking cure, 51, 52
Telepathy, 54
Thanatos, 123-24
Three Essays on the Theory of Sexuality (Freud), 90, 93, 94-95
Totem and Taboo (Freud), 22, 117-19
Transference, 98, 113

Unconscious, 86-87, 117
University of Vienna, 21, 88-89

Vienna, 12, 17, 19-20, 122-23
Vienna Psychoanalytic Society, 92-93, 105, 106-7, 108, 114, 121, 131
Vitalism, 24

Wednesday Psychological Society, 92-93, 101
Weininger, Otto, 92
"Wild Analysis" (Freud), 111-12
World War I, 121-22

Margaret Muckenhoupt is an independent psychological researcher. She holds an A.B. degree from Harvard University and a Sc.M. degree from Brown University. She has worked on clinical studies of schizophrenia and obsessive-compulsive disorder, and has performed research on color vision and psycholinguistics. She lives in Somerville, Massachusetts.

Owen Gingerich is Professor of Astronomy and of the History of Science at the Harvard-Smithsonian Center for Astrophysics in Cambridge, Massachusetts. The author of more than 400 articles and reviews, he has also written *The Great Copernicus Chase and Other Adventures in Astronomical History* and *The Eye of Heaven: Ptolemy, Copernicus, Kepler.*